D1570052

MIKE PENCE

VICE PRESIDENT OF THE UNITED STATES

Amanda Sales

E **Enslow Publishing**
101 W. 23rd Street
Suite 240
New York, NY 10011
USA
enslow.com

Dedicated to Alex, for always encouraging and supporting my dreams. Together, with you, everything is better!

Published in 2019 by Enslow Publishing, LLC.
101 W. 23rd Street, Suite 240, New York, NY 10011

Library of Congress Cataloging-in-Publication Data

Names: Sales, Amanda, author.
Title: Mike Pence : Vice President of the United States / Amanda Sales.
Description: New York, NY : Enslow Publishing, 2019. | Series: Influential lives | Includes bibliographical references and index. | Audience: Grades 7-12.
Identifiers: LCCN 2018012232| ISBN 9781978503434 (library bound) | ISBN 9781978505186 (pbk.)
Subjects: LCSH: Pence, Mike, 1959- | Vice-Presidents—United States—Biography—Juvenile literature. | Governors—Indiana—Biography—Juvenile literature. | Legislators—United States—Biography—Juvenile literature. | Conservatives—United States—Biography—Juvenile literature. | United States—Politics and government—1989—Juvenile literature.
Classification: LCC E840.8.P376 S25 2019 | DDC 973.933092 [B] —dc23
LC record available at https://lccn.loc.gov/2018012232

Printed in the United States of America

To Our Readers: We have done our best to make sure all websites in this book were active and appropriate when we went to press. However, the author and the publisher have no control over and assume no liability for the material available on those websites or on any websites they may link to. Any comments or suggestions can be sent by e-mail to customerservice@enslow.com.

Contents

Introduction

●●●●●●●●●●●●●●●●●●

Throughout the ages, countless men and women have dedicated their lives to the advancement of society. It can come through the written word, like Shakespeare's timeless sonnets and plays. It can come through scientific breakthroughs, like Benjamin Franklin's invention of bifocals and the lightning rod. It can come through the act of simple and dedicated service, like Mother Teresa's gift of prayer, comfort, and charity that reached many thousands of people. It can also come through public service, like Mike Pence and his service as a congressman, governor, and now vice president. No matter the calling or avenue, when a person dedicates his or her life to the service of others, it is a noble goal.

While many have started their life of service with a genuine heart, it is all too easy for those in the public eye to become changed by power, greed, or lust. It is the duty

●●●●●●●●●●●●●●●●●●●●●●●●●

Vice President Mike Pence is a quiet but strong force who holds one of the most powerful roles in the nation.

of America's eligible voters to elect men and women of character and dedication to public service.

Now more than ever, controversy and mistrust for our nation's leaders is causing the American people to question what they stand for and find ways to work together to create a brighter future for our children. The very nature of politics tends to create division among those of different parties or viewpoints, but with an open mind and a willing ear to listen, we can find ways to lessen the divide and strengthen the bonds that bring us together as a country.

By and large, up until he was chosen as Donald Trump's running mate, Mike Pence was a man who walked in the shadows of the big leagues of politics. Beyond taking an unpopular stance on certain controversial issues and a questionable judgment regarding campaign funds early in his political career, Pence has led a scandal-free life. That is no easy feat for a politician these days.

Pence is a decidedly conservative man, both in his personal and political life. His views on abortion, gay rights, climate change, and gun rights are controversial and cause for derision in Democratic circles but can find a comfortable home among many Republicans. As is the nature of politics, Pence has many loyal fans, but there are just as many disappointed voters who hoped for a different agenda for the White House in the 2016 presidential race.

This resource focuses on each major stage in Pence's life and his contributions to the public offices he has held. A strong but quiet force in the White House, Pence is using his platform as vice president of the United

States to advance the issues he finds most important for the country. Pence has displayed his loyalty to President Donald Trump even as others have questioned Trump's unorthodox methods. Pence has deftly smoothed out the president's rough edges and subtly reinforced the president's messages on the world stage. Regardless of party allegiance, understanding Mike Pence is important for any person interested in politics and history because he will go down in history as the forty-eighth vice president of the United States.

CHAPTER ONE

Born in a Sleepy Indiana Town

· ·

June 7, 1959, was a quiet day in the small town of Columbus, Indiana. It was a Sunday, and many of the residents were enjoying a relaxing day off. Some attended church while others spent time with their families outside in the fresh air. For Edward and Nancy Pence, this was no ordinary day. They hadn't lived in Columbus that long, having moved from Indianapolis just months earlier, but it was there that Nancy delivered her third child, a boy they named Michael Richard Pence. Little did his parents know when they brought their little bundle home that someday Michael—or Mike as he would come to be known by most—would make his way into politics and that he would end up taking on one of the most prominent public positions in the world as vice president of the United States.

At home, baby Mike joined his two older brothers, Gregory and Edward. Nancy had been raised in Chicago, where she attended an all-girls Catholic school.[1] After she met and married Edward Pence, she became a

Little did Nancy Pence know that her third son would become vice president of the United States. She and her husband raised six children and provided them love and support.

homemaker. Edward Pence Sr. was also from Chicago. Before he married Nancy, he was a second lieutenant in the Korean War (1950–1953).

Michael Richard Pence was named after his maternal grandfather, Richard Michael Cawley. His grandfather immigrated to the United States from Ireland through the famed Ellis Island in 1923 and was able to get a job as a streetcar driver with the Chicago Surface Lines. Eventually, he went from driving streetcars to driving buses, and then to working in the city of Chicago's transportation department for over forty years.[2] When he was growing up, Mike was very close to his grandfather. When his grandfather died in 1980, Mike was devastated.

While his grandfather was a wonderful role model for Mike growing up, Mike also had a deep respect for

Columbus, Indiana

Columbus, Indiana, is a town that today boasts a population of around 46,000 people. But during Mike's childhood, it was home to less than half that number. Located 46 miles (74 kilometers) south of Indianapolis, this charming town, though small, has been known for many years for its architecture. Over the years, famous architects and artists designed and built over ninety of the current structures in Columbus, and it is rated as one of the top cities in the country for innovation and architectural quality, not far behind the likes of New York City and Chicago.[3]

his father. During the Korean War, Edward Pence Sr. earned a Bronze Star, a decoration awarded to soldiers in the military who give heroic service or exemplify extraordinary achievement, but he didn't like to talk about his experiences in the war, especially with his children. The war changed Edward, as it did so many men, and after he died in 1988, a cousin told Mike that his father never stopped feeling guilty for making it home from the war when so many other soldiers he knew didn't.[4] Despite the fact that his father never shared his wartime stories with him, Mike was immensely proud of him. After the war was over and he returned home, his father worked in the gas and oil industry and ran a chain of gas stations in Indiana.

An Early Start in Service

Even as a young boy, religion was a big part of Mike's life. His parents were devout Catholics, and the family was a regular fixture at their local Catholic church. The Pence brothers served as altar boys, and that meant that for much of his youth, Mike was at church six, sometimes even seven, days a week. In this way, Mike developed an early sense of duty and morality from the religious cornerstone that would be influential for the rest of his life. Intertwined with that strong sense of spiritual responsibility was the family's social responsibility— both within and outside of the church. During his adolescence, when Mike was serving his church as an altar boy, he was also serving his community as a youth coordinator for the Bartholomew County Democrats.[5]

Growing up in the small town of Columbus afforded Mike a normal, happy childhood by all accounts. Mike and his brothers were active and full of energy. A childhood friend of Mike's once said that going over to Mike's house gave him a very different experience than he had in his own home, which was filled with sisters. "It'd be like going into another world when I'd visit Mike and see the brothers interact," he said.[6] After Mike was born, a fourth brother, Thomas, came along, and much later, two sisters, Mary and Annie.

With that energy came the expectation from his parents to use his talents well. He and both his older brothers, along with several other high school students, took turns helping two local boys with muscular dystrophy get ready every morning in an effort to ensure that the boys' family was not overwhelmed. Even with the strong support of their family, these boys, Mike and Mark Reardon, experienced the generous support of their community through this regular volunteer group, whose mission it was to alleviate some of the stress the disease took on the entire family.[7]

The Pence family identified as Irish Catholic Democrats. Mike and his brothers spent their elementary and junior high years—grades one through eight—attending St. Columba Catholic School. It was during this time that the handsome young boy with dark hair developed a taste for public speaking. While it might have been hard for little Mike to keep up with his two older brothers at first, his mother noted that he became quite the talker as a boy, and she wasn't surprised by the fact that he was drawn to giving speeches. His first competition for public speaking came in fifth grade, and he loved it. Not only did he enjoy the contest, but he also won it.[8] This spurred him on to refine his skills and compete again.

When he was a sophomore in high school, speech coach Debbie Shoultz noticed his passion and talent for public speaking. She worked with him and noted that not only did he love public speaking, but he also worked hard at it. He won numerous competitions, including taking first place in the American Legion's Indiana Oratorical Contest in 1977. Shoultz noticed that Mike also had leadership qualities, and he even talked about being

Pence developed a passion for public speaking early on in his life. His speech coach watched his talent develop and believed in his leadership qualities even while he was still in high school.

president someday. During his time under her tutelage, Mike read a book titled *Growth and Development of the Constitution*. Shoultz said, "I think he became interested in politics in high school … He read that book over and over, and it obviously had an influence on his life."[9]

Family was very important to the Pence clan. Every year at Christmastime they would travel from Columbus to Chicago to be with their relatives. The siblings loved the trips and especially enjoyed spending time with their uncle Phillip, who was a dedicated Chicago police officer.[10] Mike had great admiration for Uncle Phillip and his grandfather. When he was a young child, his grandfather took the time to help Mike learn to grow proficient in his speech. As he grew older, Mike also learned about politics from his grandfather, who spoke with great respect about men like Franklin D. Roosevelt and John F. Kennedy, which is in part why Mike came to idolize the latter. Mike's grandfather was the third of six children, and Mike's great-grandfather had been a tailor in a small village in Ireland.[11] Kennedy also was from a large Irish Catholic family.

While immigration seems to be an ever-growing issue in the country today—and one that Pence has had strong opinions about during his time as a congressman and governor—it was not without obstacles in Richard Michael Cawley's day as well. Faced with either fighting in Ireland's civil war in 1920 or fleeing to America, Mike's

> [Kennedy and I] both were raised to believe that to whom much is given, much will be required. [12]

grandfather chose to leave. But because of the conflicts going on in Ireland, hostility existed for Irish Catholics in the United States. In fact, in 1921, Congress passed an act that was intended to place aggressive restrictions on immigration.[13] Despite the roadblocks he faced, Cawley made it to Chicago and settled there, little knowing at the time that it would become his lifelong home.

World Stage

Along with immigration issues taking place before Mike was born, the world was changing in some drastic ways in the year he was born. Considering the way Mike Pence the politician has attempted to shape certain issues, it is interesting to note the changes that occurred around the time he was born.

It was in the year 1959 that President Dwight D. Eisenhower signed an act that allowed Alaska and Hawaii to become the forty-ninth and fiftieth states in the country. The television program *The Twilight Zone* first aired. The microchip, which paved the way for new technologies such as the cell phone, was invented. It was also around this time that extensive research was being done and trials were conducted for birth control pills.[14] The space race was full steam ahead in that year, with the United States launching the *Pioneer 4* spacecraft into orbit. At the same time that hundreds of millions of dollars were being spent on space exploration, the unemployment rate was at just over 5 percent.

Both growth and setbacks shaped the country over the next decade. A Cuban revolutionary leader named Fidel Castro came to power in 1959 and remained

The Bay of Pigs

The Bay of Pigs was supposed to be a secret mission that would lead to the end of Fidel Castro's rule over Cuba. John F. Kennedy was still early in his presidency and was hesitant about the mission's plans but followed the prompting of his advisors to allow a small force of soldiers to bomb Castro's air force and invade an isolated spot on Cuba known as the Bay of Pigs. The invasion was a disaster. Castro caught wind of the plan and moved his planes before the US soldiers could attack. Although US intelligence discovered this, the soldiers were given the green light to invade the island anyway, leading to over 100 men being killed and 1,100 more becoming captives of the Cuban military.

in power for forty-nine years. Two years after Mike was born, John F. Kennedy became America's second-youngest president and the military debacle known as the Bay of Pigs invasion took place. Soon after, Martin Luther King Jr. led a march on Washington, DC, that involved hundreds of thousands of people listening to his famous "I have a dream" speech.

During Mike's childhood, other events occurred as well that impacted not just him but every other American of the day. For some events, he would have been too young or unaware to recognize when they happened—like the FDA's approval of the birth control pill and the civil rights movement—but these were issues that would influence his future career. The year

One of Pence's earliest political idols, John F. Kennedy, was beloved by a nation and mourned perhaps like no other US president in history. Mike learned much about Kennedy through his grandfather.

1962 is when the Cuban missile crisis took place, which brought the United States closer to a nuclear conflict than it had ever experienced, but it was also the year the entire country watched with eager fascination as John Glenn became the first American astronaut to orbit Earth. A year later, the country mourned the death of their beloved president, John F. Kennedy—and one of Mike's early political idols—at the hands of an assassin named Lee Harvey Oswald.

As the world continued to change, Mike was growing up. From his love for public speaking to his strong family ties to his deep sense of commitment to community and religious service, he was developing an identity all his own. He knew he was on a path to greatness—he just didn't know exactly where it would lead him.

CHAPTER TWO

Faith, Marriage, and Future

· · · · · · · · · · · · · · · ·

As his senior year of high school flew by, Mike Pence began to think about a career in broadcast journalism. So he sought out the advice of Sam Simmermaker, who worked as a newscaster in Columbus. After looking over several options, Pence decided to attend Hanover College, located a mere hour's drive south of his hometown, on the edge of the Ohio River. While he continued to pursue his interest in public speaking, Pence also became involved in a fraternity. During his sophomore year, Pence was elected president of Phi Gamma Delta and enjoyed his role as a leader. Even before his election within the fraternity, Pence had always nursed the dream of running for positions of leadership—especially in public office.

During his time as Phi Gamma Delta president, Pence did his best to maintain good relationships with his fraternity brothers and the college administration

During his time at Hanover College, Pence had a spirtual awakening.

• • • • • • • • • • • • • • • • • • •

alike, which was sometimes a challenging task. One of his fraternity brothers recalls a time when the fraternity was having a party and had kegs of alcohol in the house, which was against school policy, and one of the deans of the school came to their door demanding it be handed over. Some of the members tried to hide the kegs, but it was no use. While it was typical for a single fraternity member to take the blame so the entire house would not be charged with a violation, Pence showed the dean where the alcohol was and admitted it belonged to the house.[1] The entire fraternity was punished. Whether it was Pence's conscience or his desire to remain in good standing with the school administrators that led to his choice, some of members of his fraternity didn't understand it or take his choice particularly well.

While in college, Pence began to question his faith and his greater purpose in life. He met some people around him—including one of his fraternity brothers who happened to be a Christian—who seemed to have a deeper spiritual connection with God than he had experienced during his childhood as an altar boy. His fraternity brother told Pence that it was important to have a spiritual faith that you could feel in your heart and not just wear like a piece of clothing that could be taken off. When Pence saw him wearing a cross around his neck, he told Pence, "[Y]ou have got to wear it in your heart before you wear it around your neck."[3] That thought resonated with Pence, who wanted a deeper spiritual connection than he had previously experienced. He felt that his religious life had been more focused on outward deeds than inward change of heart.

> Pence's childhood nickname was "Bubbles," and his brother claims it was because Mike was "chubby and funny."[2]

As Pence struggled to figure out his feelings regarding religion, he went through a conversion experience where he accepted Jesus Christ as his savior, which he hadn't experienced on a personal level during his years in the Catholic Church. Though he began to consider himself an evangelical, he did not cut his ties with the Catholic Church right away. He was still involved in activities within the Catholic Church, such as serving as a youth minister after his conversion. His decision caused some disappointment among his family, especially his mother. It changed everything for Pence and caused him to stand out for his change of faith and shift in political views. While he had grown up a Democrat, Pence's political views began to align more with the likes of conservative Republican president Ronald Reagan.

After Pence completed his college education and graduated with a BA in history, he was offered a job in the admissions department of Hanover College. From

Ronald Reagan

Ronald Reagan was the fortieth president of the United States and served two terms, from 1981 to 1989. Before he became a politician, he was an actor who appeared in fifty-three films. He and Mike Pence share something in common: Reagan took a job as a radio announcer after high school—except he was focused on sports while Pence focused his show on politics and community issues. Also like Pence, his political views shifted from liberal to conservative. Reagan eventually ran for and won the election to become governor of California. When he ran for president with George H. W. Bush as his running mate, he won the electoral votes by a huge margin—both in his 1980 and 1984 campaigns.

During Reagan's presidency, the country experienced rising prosperity without war or economic downturn. His proclaimed goal for the country was to restore "the great, confident roar of American progress and growth and optimism" and to promote "peace through strength."[4]

1981 to 1983, Pence worked as an admissions counselor. While there, he decided to pursue a law degree at Indiana University. Even as he wrestled with conflicted feelings regarding his childhood faith, he considered entering the priesthood for a short period of time after graduating from college.[5]

First Comes Mass, Then Comes Marriage

It was during this time of internal conflict that Pence ended up meeting a beautiful young woman at mass at

Mike and Karen Pence knew they were destined to be together and married barely a year after they first met. Karen always had a passion for helping people and enjoyed a long career in art education.

the St. Thomas Aquinas Church. Karen Batten was born in Kansas and was raised in Indiana, and she played the guitar at mass services. She was two years older than Pence and had focused her education on teaching and art. Attending Butler University, she obtained a BS and MS in elementary education. When Karen met Mike after playing guitar one evening at mass, she was already working as a teacher at a small private school in Indianapolis. She had married her high school sweetheart in 1978 and was recently divorced when she met Mike, a fact that didn't faze him. They went to an ice skating rink on their first date.[6]

Only months after they met, in August 1984, Mike proposed. Karen was as smitten as Mike. She had already engraved a cross with the word "yes" on it and carried it with her when they spent time together because she knew from early on in their relationship that she wanted to marry him. When he popped the question, she answered by giving him the cross.[7] They were married on June 8, 1985, and started their life together in Indiana.

Like many young couples, Mike and Karen began to dream about having a family after they got married, but as the months went by and Karen didn't get pregnant, she began to worry. In her late twenties when she married Mike, Karen was eager to begin her journey into motherhood. In fact, it was a role she had looked forward to her entire life. Their doctor found nothing that indicated they would not be able to have children, but still they continued to have difficulties.[8]

For six years, the couple was unable to conceive. They looked into fertility treatments and began to consider adoption. During the early years of their struggle, Karen had a hard time accepting that she might never have the family she dreamed of. Coping with infertility caused Karen's faith in God to waiver for a time. It was incredibly difficult to have friends and family around her getting pregnant when she wasn't able to conceive. She couldn't understand how God would deny her something she wanted so badly.

During this time, the couple hid their fertility struggles from even their closest friends and family. Karen admitted in an interview years later, "It can be a very heartbreaking experience, and so for us, we thought, maybe we're just not going to be a couple that has children."[9] Some people questioned why they weren't starting a family but they didn't want to burden those around them with the reality of their situation, knowing it would cause some to worry or feel concerned when hearing the news about other couples getting pregnant.

In time, Karen came to embrace the idea of adoption, though the option scared her off in the beginning. She and Mike put their names on a wait list with an adoption agency and hoped for the best. Some time later, they got a call from the adoption agency telling them that a little boy would soon be born and available for adoption. Ironically, Karen and Mike had just discovered that they were pregnant with their first child—after six long years of trying—and they chose to remove their names from the adoption list.[10] Finally, they were going to have a family of their own. Within a period of three years, the couple that thought they couldn't get pregnant went from a family of two to a family of five.

While they experienced some heartbreak during their period of infertility, Mike and Karen eventually got the family they wanted.

• • • • • • • • • • • • • • • • • • • •

As Pence's religious principles began to shift, so did his political ones. Having identified as a Democrat all his life—and one who voted for Jimmy Carter over Ronald Reagan in the 1980 presidential election—Pence's shift was surprising to his family. While they were not especially political, to move away from his religious and political roots seemed a bit drastic. But as time went on, Pence only identified more and more with the Republican Party. His conservative bent would become very pronounced over the next few years as he became involved in a run for political office.

During his time in law school, Pence developed other interests as well. He loved to draw cartoons and developed

The Dreaded LSAT

To get into law school, students must be prepared for a lot of hard work. A full-time Juris Doctor (JD) program is three years long and requires applicants to take the Law School Admissions Test (LSAT), although in rare cases some schools might accept alternative tests. This test has 175 multiple-choice questions and includes components such as reading comprehension and analytical and writing skills. Along with the LSAT, each applicant must submit letters of recommendation, a personal statement, and GPA scores. While the letters of recommendation and personal statements are important, it is more important to have a solid GPA and a good test score on the LSAT. Scores for this test range between 120 and 180, with an average being around 150. Students who get accepted into law school should be prepared to face rigorous tests, heavy research and writing, and forty to sixty hours per week dedicated to their studies.[11]

a cartoon series in the law school's paper, *Dictum*. Pence admitted that he struggled academically during his time in law school and didn't enjoy his experience. He even went so far as to say, "No one I know likes law school. It was a bad experience. I wouldn't wish it on a dog I didn't like."[12] Despite this fact, he managed to graduate in 1986.

He went into private practice at Stark Doninger Mernitz & Smith, now known as Doninger Tuohy & Bailey, but even as he practiced corporate law and was viewed as a fine associate, he had greater ambitions for himself.[13] He was only with the law firm a few years, but it was while he was still practicing that Pence decided to turn his sights on political office. Karen knew from early on in their relationship that he was determined to go into public office, and she was supportive of his ambitions.

> No one I know likes law school. It was a bad experience. I wouldn't wish it on a dog I didn't like.

Gearing up for his first political race, Pence knew it would be a tough fight, but he also knew it was something he wanted. He had worked hard to hone his skills as a public speaker in high school. He had displayed a desire to be a leader and get involved in activities through different venues of community service as a youth and fraternity president in college. He had also developed the ability to work hard and serve others during his time as an attorney. All of these skills came together as he began his first political campaign at the age of twenty-eight.

CHAPTER THREE

Plunge into the Political Pool

· · · · · · · · · · · · · · · · · · · ·

P ence was eager to begin his career in public office. Shortly before 1988, just three years after he and Karen married, Pence announced that he was going to take the plunge and run for a seat in the US House of Representatives. It seemed like a bold move for a man not even thirty years old, but Pence was ready to move into the next chapter of his life and knew that it was no time to be timid if he wanted to reach greatness.

While Karen Pence was supportive of her husband's goal, not everyone in the family was happy about his decision. Edward Pence was upset that his son was going into politics when he was newly married and had a good job. Over the Christmas holidays in the days before 1988, Edward approached Mike and voiced his disappointment and concerns. He even got one of Mike's older brothers to join in the fray and try to convince him that he was making a big mistake.

Congress Calls

Pence listened to their concerns and then returned with his own arguments. Eventually, his father came around to the idea. Edward Jr., the brother recruited to discourage Mike from his mission, said of his father, "In fact he became a big supporter and was really helpful in coaching Mike on raising money for the campaign. He took Mike throughout the district and introduced him to all the acquaintances he had made in his business career. It was invaluable."[1] It meant the world to Pence that his father came to understand his drive to become a congressman. The strong, close-knit family revealed that they would continue to support each other through any changes and obstacles.

Edward Sr. went beyond just introducing him to business associates. He had signs made for Pence's campaign that could be placed in the yards of supporters, and he became a strong source of support and encouragement for Pence. While he had reservations about his son making a life in politics, he ultimately wanted his children to be happy and face their own challenges with dignity and courage. When Edward Sr. passed away from a heart attack in April 1988, the family was devastated. In the wake of the loss, Pence continued to fight hard in the final months before the election. His family, taking an example from their great patriarch, stepped up to help as well. Ed Jr. and his brother Greg took all the signs still left that their father had made and ensured that every last one was placed.[2]

Pence won the nomination for the Republican Party for the US House seat in Indiana's 2nd district, but he

Congress

Congress is made up of two branches: the US House of Representatives and the Senate. These two branches come together to create and amend legislation. It is often referred to as the bicameral US Congress, with the House of Representatives comprising the lower chamber and the Senate comprising the upper chamber. The House of Representatives and the Senate are equal in their power but they do have different structures, and they each carry out different roles within the legislative process. The House of Representatives elects a total of 435 members, and each member serves for two years. The Senate elects only fifty members—two for each state—and each member serves for six years. All members serving in Congress are appointed by elections of the people. The number of members in the House of Representatives is determined by the number of people in the state in which they were elected; it is for this reason that California has fifty-three representatives while Nebraska has only three.[3]

lost the race to the Democratic veteran, Congressman Phil Sharp. During the race, Pence employed tactics that attacked Sharp's character and leadership abilities. In a two-page brochure mailed to thousands of voters, Team Pence showed images of a razor blade, cash formed in a tight roll, and white powder—to indicate cocaine use—on page one. The caption beside it held these words:

Pence lost two congressional races to Phil Sharp (*left*), a Democrat. Pence's tactics were aggressive and downright dirty at times.

• •

"There's Something Phil Sharp Isn't Telling You About His Record on Drugs…." Page two revealed the follow-up caption in letters formed by white powder: "It's Weak."[4]

Pence rolled out his bullet-point plan for fighting against drugs while also stating that his opponent's plan was weak and ineffective. He implied that Sharp was only interested in serving the needs of those who lined his pockets. Pence strove to appear like a man of the people, even riding his bike through the county with Karen so they could spend time talking with voters. In a newspaper article featuring Pence, he noted that he had a special appreciation for those who have struggled in life and felt he could relate because of his own struggles as a self-described "chubby, unpopular child." He said, "I've never forgot what it's like to be in that position, to be looked down upon because I was fat or a fourth-string center or in shop class. Having to go through that has taught me that every person in this world has value, no matter what their position or status. I'll never forget that."[5]

Unfortunately, his aggressive campaigning didn't make enough of an impression on the public. While this was a blow, Pence was anxious to try again. In 1990, he launched another campaign, running against Phil Sharp for the second time. To ensure that he would be wholly focused on his campaign, Pence quit his job and dedicated all of his time to the race. Karen was still working as a teacher, and their children hadn't come along yet, but losing Pence's income did make things more difficult on the couple financially.

> "Every person in this world has value, no matter what their position or status."

Confessions of a Negative Campaigner

In both his 1988 and 1990 campaigns, Pence implied that Sharp was accepting money from people with special interests who would promote their own agendas and inhibit Sharp from making the best choices for the people. These accusations blew up in Pence's face when a dirty little secret was exposed regarding the funds his own team received. Since quitting his full-time job to focus solely on the race, Pence had used thousands

Pence met with President Ronald Reagan during his campaign for Congress in 1988. He greatly admired Reagan and expressed that the experience talking with the president was rather surreal.

●●●●●●●●●●●●●●●●●●●●●●

of dollars of campaign money to pay for everything from his mortgage to his wife's car payment to golf tournament fees. Spending political donations on such personal needs was not actually illegal at the time, but it was considered unethical. It also made people lose faith in Pence.

While he had a real shot at winning the 1990 election before the campaign funds revelation, his opponent seized the opportunity to make sure Pence wouldn't win this fight. Sharp's team made it very clear that Pence was hypocritical and unethical. They got his finance reports

Political Campaigns

Coordinating political campaigns involves huge amounts of time and money and can only happen with lots of help. Campaigns can take place at the local, state, and federal levels. Methods of reaching voters can range from mailing fliers; buying advertising space on television, radio, newspapers, and other venues; making phone calls; debating; and even going door to door. The main goal of a campaign is to persuade people to vote for their candidate because he or she is the best person for the job. Candidates create slogans (or one of their dozens of team members do) intended to convey who they are and what they stand for. Barack Obama's was "Change we can believe in." Franklin D. Roosevelt's slogan was "Happy days are here again." Ronald Reagan's is especially interesting: "Let's make America great again." It differs by just a single word from the 2016 slogan of Donald Trump.

and informed the public that they were helping to pay the Pence's bills if they had given money in support of his campaign. The way Pence handled the situation made it even worse. Rather than apologize or recognize why it caused such concern among voters, Pence simply told reporters that he needed the money since taking a large pay cut when he quit his job, adding, "I'm not embarrassed that I need to make a living."[6]

Angry that Sharp had found a solid issue to attack, Pence resorted to more negative strategies as the race continued. He allowed his campaign to spread a rumor that Sharp was selling his family farm to be used as a nuclear waste dump site. On top of that, Pence ran a television ad that offended a large number of people, especially those of Arab American descent. The ad featured a man dressed in a robe and sunglasses meant to reflect traditional Arab fashion. The man in the ad thanked Phil Sharp for his part in keeping trade going between the United States and foreign oil companies. Even the Indiana editorial board was disgusted with the method of Pence's campaigning and denounced the ad.[7]

It came as no surprise that Pence lost the race again in 1990. His misuse of political contributions caused the Democratic Congressional Campaign Committee to file a complaint with the Federal Election Commission (FEC). While no actions were taken against Pence, the complaints led to new rules regarding how candidates could spend campaign funds and banned any personal use of those funds.[8]

It was another bitter pill for Pence to swallow. It took some time for him to reflect and learn from the experience, but a year after his defeat, he penned a personal apology to Phil Sharp. He also wrote an article in which he confessed that his negative methods of campaigning were wrong. Pence's article, "Confessions of a Negative Campaigner," showed up in the *Indiana Policy Review* in October 1991. It discussed why negative campaigning is wrong and examined the reasons politicians fall so easily into the mode of such a campaign.

Pence revealed one of his biggest regrets regarding his party's defeat in the article, saying that it seemed

Thanks to Pence, the Federal Election Commission developed new rules and procedures regarding how candidates could spend campaign funds.

• • • • • • • • • • • • • • • • • • • •

"grievous that the faithful were left with so few clues as to how I would have governed differently."[9] Because he dumped so much negative energy into the fight, he realized that the positive attributes he could have contributed to Congress went unseen. He went on to note three pieces that are crucial for a good campaign: one, "a campaign ought to demonstrate the basic human decency of the candidate"; two, "a campaign ought to be about the advancement of issues whose success or failure is more significant than that of the candidate"; and three, "campaigns should be about winning."[10]

In 1991, Pence went to work for the Indiana Review Policy Foundation, and by the time he wrote

> "A campaign ought to be about the advancement of issues whose success or failure is more significant than that of the candidate."

"Confessions of a Negative Campaigner" he was already president of the foundation. Created by Byron S. Lamm in 1989, the nonprofit was intended to be a think tank where ideas could be shared on government, economics, and education. Pence spent roughly three years at the think tank. In 1992, he overlapped his job as president of the Indiana Policy Review with a radio program called *The Mike Pence Show*. In 1993, he moved on to pursue his career in radio full-time.

Yet another chapter began for Pence as he transitioned into radio broadcasting. His family was expanding, and it seemed he decided to put his political aspirations on the back burner. He knew full well he would return to his goal of getting elected to public office down the road, but in the meantime he was happy where he was.

CHAPTER FOUR

The Developing Communicator

· ·

The months that followed Pence's failed 1990 election were busy. Mike and Karen Pence had three children in quick succession. He enjoyed his leadership role as president of the Indiana Policy Review Foundation while Karen juggled her role as a new mother and elementary school teacher. Their life in Indianapolis was full and happy.

After Pence had been working at the Indiana Policy Review Foundation for some months, Sharon Disinger, a woman who owned a small radio station with her husband in Rushville, Indiana, contacted him to discuss a proposition. She had watched his race and knew his style of communicating and connecting with people. They talked on the phone for a few minutes before Disinger revealed the reason for her call. She was eager to give Pence a time slot at her radio station to cohost a small show. Even with his two failed attempts to enter the world of politics, Disinger believed he would do very well in the radio game. He had an easy, engaging way of talking to people and came across as polite and caring. Even though Pence had stooped low with his campaigning methods in his 1990 race, his personal demeanor was pleasant and respectful. Ashamed of the tactics he employed during the campaign, Pence seemed determined to turn over a new leaf.

The Mike Pence Show

Pence drove out to meet with Disinger and her husband and discuss the details of the proposed show. They settled on an agreement to have Pence cohost a one-hour weekly radio program that focused on policies and politics. With Pence's background in public speaking and law, not to mention brief foray into politics with his two campaigns, it seemed like a perfect fit.

In short time, Pence knew he had found a new career path for the foreseeable future. He loved talking about current political issues, and he loved talking with callers. Disinger noted that some callers would get angry or unpleasant but that the tone in the 1990s was far less hostile than it is today. Even with sharp political differences "[p]eople didn't seem as angry then. People didn't feel the need to yell and scream."[1] And even when some people would voice their opinions in disrespectful ways, Pence was good at maintaining his own control. Whether it was lessons he learned from the negative impact his campaign had on others or that he was maturing, it appeared that Pence became good at employing principles of decency and kindness on the program.

1993

In 1993, the same year Pence started his daily radio show, Bill Clinton was inaugurated as the forty-second president of the United States. Barely a month after Clinton took office, the North Tower of the World Trade Center was bombed, killing six people and injuring over one thousand. In the same year, Clinton signed a bill into law that required anyone buying a handgun to pass a background check. It was called the Brady Handgun Violence Prevention Act. He also responded to the attempted assassination of former president George H. W. Bush while in Kuwait by directing a missile attack on Iraqi intelligence headquarters in Baghdad. Clinton also rolled out his "Don't Ask, Don't Tell" policy for homosexuals in the military. This policy banned the military from discriminating against men and women who were closeted or perceived homosexuals, but it still allowed an openly homosexual person to be discharged from military service. The law remained in effect until 2011.

Eventually Pence decided to quit his job at the Indiana Policy Review Foundation and make *The Mike Pence Show* his main focus. He found a bigger network that was able to give him a three-hour weekday morning show. With a starting number of six radio stations airing his program every morning, Pence developed a platform for himself to connect with people from all walks of life. Perhaps he also recognized the opportunity to redeem his image and show people that in spite of his desperate and hostile campaign, he was reformed and desired to do better.

The style Pence developed on his show was personable and direct. His conservative opinions resonated with a lot of people, and for those who didn't agree with his stance on issues, it created interesting discussions and debates. He made it a point to listen to those who called in and respect their viewpoint even if he disagreed. While discussion and debate were a large part of his show, the goal was certainly not to create conflict for conflict's sake. After debating with a caller, Pence would often end by saying, "We'll just have to agree to disagree."[2]

Pence's goal to expand his radio career happened when he eventually worked his way into twenty radio

Pence went from cohosting a weekly radio program to developing his own daily show. This platform allowed him to share ideas, connect with people, and discuss current political news.

stations, which resulted in an audience that reached the span of the entire state of Indiana. He sometimes described himself as "Rush Limbaugh on decaf," which was a fairly good comparison considering that Limbaugh was a seasoned conservative radio talk show host who discussed politics.[3] Limbaugh broadcasted from New York City and had already established a large following for his

> "We'll just have to agree to disagree."

pointed, edgy style. It was evident that Pence was not as combative and aggressive in his opinions as Limbaugh, but he still had no problem expressing his point of view. Pence's successor, Greg Garrison, said of Pence that his "calming but yet authoritative voice was what made him popular."[4]

Over the course of his time on the radio, Pence covered dozens of different topics. On one show he discussed how a particular case of military discharge was handled. A young woman named Kelly Flinn—the first female B-52 pilot in the US Air Force—had been caught engaging in an affair with a subordinate's husband. Such actions are not condoned by the military, and Flinn was told to terminate her relationship with the married man immediately. When her superiors discovered that she hadn't followed orders to terminate the relationship, and then lied about her actions under oath, they chose to discharge her from the Air Force.

Because of the controversy that surrounded this case at the time, it boosted Flinn into the limelight. Rather

Pence called himself a milder version of Rush Limbaugh, who was a much more combative radio host than Pence.

• •

than face a negative charge, Flinn was given a general discharge, which meant that she could still receive most benefits given to honorably discharged soldiers and that she was not found negligent in the performance of her duties. Some felt the treatment of this case was unfair, as the trial came about in large part because of infidelity, but others saw her punishment as not harsh enough. The media took the story and viewed it from the angle of adultery. But the real issue of the trial was about Flinn's insubordination and dishonesty. According to General Ronald Fogleman, "This is an issue about an officer entrusted to fly nuclear weapons who disobeyed an order, who lied. That's what this is about."[5]

Pence opened the lines to callers asking their opinions about the trial and outcome. He argued that the media was only focusing on the issue of adultery—implying that adultery was not an action that the military or any institution should punish—and that the affair was not the only thing that caused Flinn's military demise. He added that he found it disconcerting that adultery didn't seem to be considered a big offense anymore, positioning that the character of a person mattered and adultery revealed a slip in character.[6] Additionally, he argued that in other

The Indy 500

Indianapolis is proud of the fact that it hosts one of the greatest spectator sports in the United States. The Indianapolis 500 is held every year at the Indianapolis Motor Speedway, which boasts a track that is 2.5 miles (4 kilometers) and shaped like a boxy oval. Each of the thirty-three cars in the race drive around the track two hundred times to make a total of 500 miles (805 km). The first race was held in 1911, and the event has continued every year since then.

The Indianapolis Motor Speedway can seat up to 250,000 people. The cars in the Indy500 are open cockpit and can reach speeds of around 230 miles (370 km) per hour. It is tradition to give the winner of the race a bottle of milk to celebrate their win. This started in 1933, when the winner requested a glass of buttermilk after he won and made the same request three years later. Ever since then, the winner has been given a bottle of milk after a win.

cases, harsher punishments were doled out. Regardless of rank or media attention, such an offense should be punished in the same way.

Sometimes Pence used his show to talk about lighter issues. He talked about the Indy500 race, an event that he relished and attended regularly. He talked about local issues like the state fair and high school sports. On one show broadcast before Memorial Day weekend, he talked about his respect for those in uniform; he reminded his listeners of the special commemoration that would take place over the weekend; and he devoted the final three minutes of his show to expressing his deep appreciation to all who had served.[8]

> We are committed to running a positive, issues-oriented campaign.[7]

Third Time's a Charm

In 1999, after spending six years in radio, Pence decided it was time to try another run for Congress. The current Republican congressman in his district gave up his seat to run for governor, and Pence jumped at his chance. Because of his popular radio show, Pence was a minor celebrity, at least to those within the state of Indiana. He was likeable and friendly and had further developed his communication skills.

The approach Pence took for the 2000 campaign was definitely different than his previous two campaigns. He had matured from a newly married young man who was green to the political scene to a mature family man who was now just past forty years old and had much more world experience. One television ad featured Pence speaking to the camera in a soft, soothing tone, explaining why he would be a good fit for the congressional seat. He alluded to his earlier campaigns by saying that he realized negative and personal attacks on opponents had no place in a political career. With his silver hair and calm brown eyes, Pence assured his audience that he would focus on the issues and what he could do for the people of Indiana rather than waste time on what his opponent wouldn't do.[9]

Pence won the Congressional seat by focusing his campaign on helping middle-class families create better lives for their children.

Another ad showed clips of Pence with his family as he spoke this message: "Our nation is in need of renewal as never before. We must renew the American dream and I believe we can. By lifting the burden of taxes off families, small businesses, and family farms so they can once again dream and build a better life for their children. By rebuilding the military after years of Clinton cutbacks and reasserting the Constitutional rule of law and the right to life. Why am I running for Congress? To renew the dream of a strong and good America."[10] His rhetoric for the 2000 election seemed similar to the platform he and Donald Trump would use later in the presidential election of 2016, with a focus on how the American dream needed to be restored.

This time around, Pence won the election. Showing the public a grounded, patriotic family man seemed to give the public faith in his message. He left his radio show in the hands of Greg Garrison and dove eagerly into his new role representing the 2nd congressional district of Indiana in the United State House of Representatives. New and uncharted territory lay ahead of Pence, and he was eager to prove himself capable of the new position.

CHAPTER FIVE

Quiet Rebel

· · · · · · · · · · · · · · · · · ·

I n January 2001, Mike Pence officially began his term in the United States House of Representatives. The new congressman wasted no time jumping into the fray and voicing his opinions, happily debating and pushing the issues he felt were important to his community. One of the main duties of US representatives is to introduce bills and try to pass legislation that will benefit their district. They sit on committees to discuss proposed changes and have meetings with various types of people to gain a deeper understanding of the needs within their district. That could mean meeting with businessmen, lobbyists, teachers, school boards, and other politicians. They attend social events and spend time trying to help their district find ways to raise money and take advantage of available government funds for important causes.

The duties of his position kept Pence busy. He focused on many issues but especially those regarding education, foreign affairs, agriculture, and international relations. He was reelected to Congress six times, carving out a niche for himself as "a Christian, a conservative and a Republican, in that order."[1] His colleagues expressed their admiration for him as a decent man who stood by his values even when they weren't popular.

Comfortable in Opposition

Early on, Pence stood against a few proposed bills that had strong bipartisan support. The first of those was the No Child Left Behind Act proposed by President George W. Bush in 2001. As it happens in most cases, debate and deliberation surrounded this bill, but in the end it passed by a large majority. Although it might have been tempting to give way to pressure and join the large number voting for the bill, Pence seemed comfortable with his decision to oppose it.

> "I'm a Christian, a conservative, and a Republican—in that order."

The No Child Left Behind Act (NCLB) was a broad plan that was intended to create more accountability in schools all across the country, as well as provide disadvantaged students with a stronger support system for their learning needs. It encouraged standards-based reforms in education. After NCLB was passed, every state was required to have students take tests in every grade between third and eighth, and then again each year in high school. The goal in 2002 when the bill became law

Pence was in the minority that opposed George W. Bush's No Child
Left Behind Act.

• •

was to ensure that all students would meet or exceed the
standards set by each state by 2014.[2]

The four foundational points of NCLB were
accountability, flexibility, research-based education,
and parent options. The bill asserted that accountability
would mean that all students deserved access to a solid
education, including those who were in disadvantaged
areas, and that faculty within the school would be held
to higher standards to ensure this was happening.
Flexibility would mean that schools would have some
freedom to choose how to spend federal education

funds. With the promise of research-based education, the act meant to highlight how innovative techniques would be employed to give students the best education possible, focusing on methods backed by science. The fourth goal of parent options was to provide parents with more options for their children in terms of where they would go to school, especially if the standards of a district were not met multiple years in a row.[3]

While it would be unlikely to find anyone who opposed the ideals within NCLB, a small number of members within Congress felt that the bill would not be able to actually deliver on its goals. One of the reasons Pence opposed the bill is because he was a firm believer in keeping government power in check, thus allowing state and local communities to control their business better. He thought that the federal government should have a smaller role in many areas, including education.

In the coming years, many people were critical of NCLB, saying that it put heavy pressure on teachers to "teach to the test."[4] It was designed in such a way that when a school didn't meet the state standards, the people within the school—students and faculty alike—seemed to suffer the most. If a school failed to meet the standards after five to six years consecutively, measures were taken to restructure and reform the school, which sometimes even meant shutting down the troubled school altogether. Naturally, this caused concern among many parents and school faculty. Sometimes when a school was shut down, the students were redirected to schools that did not fit their needs or were harder to attend because of the distance.

During Pence's time as a congressman, he sponsored dozens of bills. A number of them involved a requested suspension of taxation on certain drugs. He also introduced bills that ranged from the prevention of child pornography to abortion prevention to the right to freely express political views.[5] However, none of the bills that Pence sponsored were ever made into laws. Beyond those he sponsored, he argued for or against and voted on dozens more, hoping that his voice would leave an impression on those within his party and even those outside of it.

Pence voted against the Medicare prescription drug expansion proposed by President Bush in 2002.

During his time in Congress, Pence was active in sponsoring dozens of bills and voting on dozens more. None of his sponsored bills passed into law, but he sought to make a difference in his role.

Chairman of the House

In the final months of 2008, Mike Pence ran for the position of chairman of the House Republican Conference and worked closely with John Boehner, the Republican Party leader who had first suggested that he try for the position. Later Boehner said that working with Pence was "one of the best decisions I made. Pence and his team were constant sources of support and good counsel."[6] As the chairman of the House, Pence presided over meetings and acted in a leadership position within the Republican Party.

Medicare is a health insurance plan for seniors who are sixty-five years old and above and some people with disabilities. The federal government provides Medicare as an option for seniors choosing their health care, and it is intended to be more affordable than private plans. For many seniors who spend large amounts of money on prescription drugs every year, President Bush's Medicare reform plan was intended to offer them some relief from paying full price for all of their prescription drugs.

As with his opposition to NCLB, Pence believed that the federal government needed to be limited in its power. Regarding entitlements like Medicare, he favored less government involvement and more privatization.[7] From Pence's point of view, the bill that President Bush proposed was unwise and not in the best interest of the American people. He felt it would be too costly, with a price tag of a whopping $400 million or more.[8] While

Pence and other conservatives in Congress felt that the bill would cost too much, Democrats on the other side of the issue believed that more needed to be done to help low-income seniors.

Pence felt so strongly about ensuring that the bill wouldn't pass that he gathered other like-minded Republicans together before the vote to encourage them to stay strong in their opposition. Unfortunately for Pence, some of his fellow Republicans caved to the pressure their party felt to stand behind their Republican commander in chief, and the bill passed.

In 2004 and 2005, Pence partnered with Democratic representative Rick Boucher to sponsor a bill focused on protecting journalists from prosecution for refusing to reveal their sources, which would essentially work to ensure the freedoms promised by the First Amendment. While the nature of Pence's work exposed him to more scrutiny by the media than the average American, he believed in a strong and independent press, even when that very press often spun reports in unfair or unflattering lights. The eventual development of the Free Flow of Information Act never passed, but it reflected Pence's ideals on lessening the grip of big government.

In 2006, Pence spearheaded a bill that focused on immigration reform. His proposed bill would give undocumented immigrants a chance to begin the process toward citizenship. While the bill did not pass, many in his own party were disappointed by the very introduction of Pence's bill, feeling that it was a betrayal to their party values.[9] Others, including President Bush, applauded the bill and helped Pence maintain hope that it would pave the way for additional immigration reform in the future.

Wall Street Bailout Crisis

In 2007–2008, the US economy was beginning to falter. Hundreds and even thousands of people were losing their jobs as the country fell into a full-blown financial crisis. On September 15, 2008, a global investment bank, Lehman Brothers, filed for bankruptcy and collapsed. Lehman Brothers and other massive banks had been incorporating aggressive risks into their regular business practices, leading to their eventual demise.

Up until 2008, banks were approving high mortgages to large numbers of home buyers. This resulted in housing prices going up. It allowed people to get comfortable borrowing more money from the bank

Free Press

An alarming trend developed around the time Pence and Boucher first starting crafting the Free Flow of Information Act. Journalists were being coerced into revealing their sources, with some being threatened or thrown into jail. Pence spoke out against these incidents and continued to work toward enacting a law that would shield those in the media for such practices. Pence declared, "Concentrations of power should be subject to greater scrutiny. I just think that it is imperative that we preserve the transparency of the American government. And the only way you can do that is by preserving a free and independent press."[10]

than they reasonably should have, or else borrow against their homes for cash. Both scenarios created a dangerous bubble in which people felt safe where they actually were not. Because people were borrowing up to their credit limits, when they ended up experiencing any hardship that caused them to become delinquent in their repayment to the bank, the results were tragic. Thousands of people lost their homes to foreclosures or evictions. These delinquencies began happening in higher numbers in 2006 and only increased from there. By the time 2008 rolled around, the financial stability of large banks was gone and started the chain reaction leading to the bankruptcy of Lehman Brothers.

Politicians in Congress immediately began to work on a plan that would help lessen the blow of the crisis. Congress proposed a $700 billion bailout for the other banks on Wall Street that were dangerously close to following in the footsteps of Lehman Brothers. Many Americans were outraged that the country's leaders could find a way to bail out the richest banks in the country—especially when those same banks displayed reckless, selfish behavior that led to the crisis in the first place—when they seemed to find it so hard to pass laws that would benefit the average American. In all reality, the $700 billion would be coming out of the American taxpayer pockets.[11]

Pence was opposed to the Wall Street bailout from its inception. The Emergency Economic Stabilization Act was formed and resulted in the Troubled Asset Relief Program (TARP). When a revised plan was proposed, Pence was opposed to that as well. He asserted his

Pence believed that giving power to the government to distribute billions to sinking corporations violated American ideals and would ultimately hurt the American people.

• • • • • • • • • • • • • • • • • • • •

opinion on why the bailout was a bad idea in a letter to his colleagues in Congress. "The decision to give the federal government the ability to nationalize almost every bad mortgage in America interrupts this basic truth of our free market economy. Republicans improved this bill but it remains the largest corporate bailout in American history, forever changes the relationship between government and the financial sector, and passes the cost along to the American people."[12] At the heart of his argument was, once again, the principle that increasing government power opposed the ideals of the Founding Fathers and certainly was not in the best interest of the American people. He said, "I did not come to Washington to expand the size and scope of government. I did not come to Washington to ask working Americans to subsidize the bad decisions of corporate America."[13]

> **"I did not come to Washington to expand the size and scope of government."**

As his sixth term as a US representative began to wind down, Pence realized that he wanted a new challenge. He campaigned all over the state of Indiana and won the title of governor of Indiana in 2012. Suddenly time seemed to have flown by, and Pence was a fifty-three-year-old father with three children who were quickly nearing adulthood. Once more, he moved his family back to Indiana as he prepared to begin yet another new chapter in his life.

CHAPTER SIX

From Tax Cuts to Abortion Reform

On January 14, 2013, Mike Pence became the fiftieth governor of Indiana. He experienced a tight race against Democrat John R. Gregg and Libertarian Rupert Boneham but was victorious in the end. One of the first items on Pence's to-do list as governor was to have his congressional papers sealed, which meant that they would be unavailable to the public until the year 2022 or his death. He and his wife, Karen, moved into the governor's mansion just after he took office, and their youngest daughter, Audrey, lived with them until that fall when she went off to college. Pence's two older children had already moved out and started their adult lives, with Michael Jr. enjoying his time as a college student at Purdue and their older daughter, Charlotte, going to college at DePaul University. The governor's mansion, a 10,000-square-foot (930-square-meter) home located in Indianapolis, had been vacant during the eight years the previous governor was in office, but it became the

Pence became the fiftieth Governor of Indiana on January 14, 2013, as his family stood witness. One of the top orders of business for Governor Pence was to focus on improving Indiana's economy.

• •

setting of numerous social and political gatherings after the Pences moved in.

Economic Considerations

Pence focused on many issues during his time as governor, but near the top of the list was his concern for Indiana's economy. He had conservative plans for the state's budget. While the previous governor had left Indiana with a large budget reserve of $2 billion, Pence decided to add to the reserve. To do this, he cut funding to multiple agencies, including Family and Social Services and the Department of Correction.[1] At the same time he cut funding, Pence signed a law that allowed for business owners to determine whether or not they would give raises or offer benefits to their employees beyond those required by federal law. Some people wanted Pence to step in and force wage increases, believing that it would help Indiana residents. But just as Pence opposed raising the minimum wage during his time as a representative, he still held to the belief that doing so would actually hurt the working poor.[2]

While Pence didn't want to force wage increases, he did work to cut state taxes. He vetoed a local tax law in the summer of 2013 that would have increased the taxes of residents, but the House of Representatives overrode the veto.[3] Even as Pence worked to balance the budget, the state's economy was slow. In 2014, two large companies, Carrier Corporation and United Technologies Electronics Controls, relocated away from Indiana and caused over two thousand people to lose their jobs.

Though people were frustrated by the fact that the average wage in Indiana was below the national average and the economy was sluggish, this couldn't be contributed entirely to one man. An issue that people could and did blame Pence for was his signing of the Religious Freedom Restoration Act in 2015. The Religious Freedom Restoration Act (RFRA) was a bill that would allow business owners to deny services to people in the name of their religion. Pence had long believed, and expressed, that homosexuality is not condoned based on his religious principles, but many argued that the bill he signed would enable discrimination against those within the LGBT community. Those opposed to the law felt that Pence's personal religious principles should not

NCLB

At its outset, No Child Left Behind was strongly supported by Congress and many within the education realm. Many of its advocates later shifted their opinion of the act. Diane Ravitch is a former assistant secretary of education who wrote a book expressing her disappointment in NCLB. She wrote that putting pressure on students to pass standardized tests increased the amount of cheating and statistical manipulation. Rather than building up students and school districts, NCLB was creating an environment of punishment for those who didn't reach the standards. "Instead of raising standards it's actually lowered standards because many states have 'dumbed down' their tests or changed the scoring of their tests to say more kids are passing than actually are." She argued that the best way for the federal government to help was to allow those at the ground level—such as teachers and administrators—to choose the best solutions for their local education issues.[4]

make their way into public policies. According to Pence, RFRA was meant to provide protection to business owners who did not feel comfortable extending service to same-sex couples due to their biblical beliefs.

In very short order, hundreds and thousands of people came out against RFRA, expressing concern that it set a dangerous precedent. Organizations such as Apple and Salesforce.com spoke out condemning the law and pledged that they would move their businesses out of Indiana altogether if it were not changed.[5] In an interview with ABC's George Stephanopoulos, Pence was asked multiple times if the law was meant to discriminate against LGBTQ groups and what he would say to those who stated emphatically that it opened the door to discrimination. Pence skirted the questions each time.[6] Within a few weeks time, Pence did concede to revise the law, which now included language that expressly prohibited discrimination. But the damage had been done, leaving plenty of Indiana citizens angry.

Thousands of people protested against Pence's Religious Freedom Restoration Act in 2015, compelling the governor to revise the law.

Religious Faith as Basis for Public Policy

Deeply intertwined with Pence's role as a political leader was his religious faith. In recent years his conservative beliefs have clashed with mainstream political policies beyond just his passing of the RFRA. Another issue that brought harsh criticism down on Pence was his stance on abortion. As governor, Pence signed a bill into

> "I'm pro-life and I don't apologize for it."[7]

law that prohibited abortion based on the fetus's gender, race, or a known abnormality.[8] Protests sprung up in opposition to the bill, and a federal court declared that it was unconstitutional and thus would not take effect as an Indiana law. While Pence stood behind his intention to protect the rights of an unborn child with his anti-abortion views, Judge Tanya Pratt ruled that a woman, not the state, has a right to make the choice about having an abortion—at least up until around twenty-four weeks when the fetus is considered viable outside the womb.[9]

Education and Drug Reform

As governor, Pence took a special interest in the state's education system. In May 2013, Pence signed the House Enrolled Act 1003, which would provide low-income families with more school options for their kids. For example, a student with disabilities who was attending or was even within the district of an F-rated school could receive a voucher toward a better school—often a private or charter school.[10] The voucher program in Indiana is one of the biggest in the country, serving over fifteen thousand students as of 2015, up from nine thousand the year before.[11] While the goal was to ensure quality education, some criticized the program for its lengthy regulations. One educational researcher complained that the heavy regulations in the program canceled out the benefits of having additional options, coming out with the question, "What's the point of school choice if the choice schools have to do many of the same things public schools do?"[12] Pence also added publicly funded preschool programs for low-income families. He released Common Core as the standard for Indiana schools in the hopes of creating standards within the state. Indiana was the first state to drop Common Core standards from its school system.

In addition to increasing the voucher program and preschool assistance for low-income families, Pence decided to shift control of the Educational Employment Relations from Glenda Ritz, Indiana's superintendent of public instruction, to people he chose personally. Glenda Ritz had acted as a go-between for the teacher unions and school boards, and she was not pleased when Pence took the position away from her. One of the issues Pence and Ritz disagree on was standardized testing, as well as how to handle the issue of students identifying as transgender—and whether to treat them in accordance with their identified gender or biological gender.[13]

Many other issues arose during Governor Pence's time in office. When President Obama rolled out his Clean Power Plan, Pence strongly opposed it and declared that Indiana would not comply with the plan,

During his time as governor, Pence focused on education reform. Having been a teacher for many years, Karen Pence also took a special interest in promoting education reforms.

• •

as it would harm the coal industry in the state. And while he had advocated for changes in immigration law during his time as a congressman, he was decidedly against allowing Syrian refugees to seek resettlement in Indiana during the Syrian refugee crisis. When Pence tried to cut funding from a refugee resettlement agency that was helping Syrians, a federal judge ruled his actions unconstitutional.

Pence is a long-time supporter of the rights of gun owners, in keeping with the Second Amendment. As governor, he signed three bills into law that favored a conservative stance on gun control, including one that allowed gun owners to carry firearms in their cars while on school property.[14] He believed that allowing citizens to arm themselves made communities safer and argued that punishing parents who chose to conceal carry while picking up their kids from school would be unfair.

Cracking down on drug use and distribution was also on Pence's agenda. The war on drugs has raged for years in the United States, but as governor Pence threw his support toward keeping heavy penalties in place for drug offenders in Indiana. While some states like Washington and Colorado were legalizing marijuana, Pence maintained his intention to fight hard against weakening drug policies. Arguments arose that legalizing

Governor Pence enjoyed time with his family during a parade in 2013. A strong family man, Pence values the deep bond he has with each of his children.

marijuana would bring revenue to the state and also keep many small-time drug offenders out of prison, but Pence didn't waver in his stance. During his second race for governor in 2016, before he pulled out to team up with Donald Trump for the presidential race, Pence declared, "I think this legislation, as it moves forward, should still seek to continue to send a way strong message to the people of Indiana and particularly to those who would come into our state to deal drugs, that we are tough and we're going to stay tough on narcotics."[15]

HIV

Human immunodeficiency virus (HIV) is a virus that destroys the body's immune system, which is critical to a person's ability to fight off infection and disease. It cannot be passed through casual contact with another individual, such as sharing a hug, kiss, or being in the vicinity of a person's sneeze. HIV can only be transmitted through certain body fluids and is most commonly passed from one person to another through unprotected sexual contact or shared drug needles. Because drug abusers often use a needle to inject drugs directly into their bloodstream for a quicker high, they are more likely to act recklessly and use a needle that has not been properly sterilized. HIV cannot be cured, but modern medical breakthroughs have found ways to control the virus and sometimes slow it enough so that it does not reach the most severe stage of infection, which is AIDS.

Even as Pence fought to keep the laws tough for drug offenders, he opposed the needle-exchange program that was proposed in 2015 after an uptick in drug users turning up positive for HIV. The needle-exchange program was controversial and had not been legal in Indiana for some time, but it allowed drug users to exchange their dirty needles for clean ones at specific locations. This program was intended to decrease infections that spread easily by drug users who shared needles. One of the biggest threats was the HIV virus. Planned Parenthood was one of the locations people could go to exchange their needles in a safe space. Pence was the driving force behind numerous Planned Parenthood locations closing, as it was his belief that the program might encourage continued drug use, or at minimum, not deter people.

When those in the health care industry discovered that a high number of people were diagnosed with HIV in late 2014 and early 2015, they notified authorities and it suddenly became an outbreak that demanded the attention of the governor. Even though he was personally opposed to the exchange program, after sitting down with multiple officials and experts, Pence knew he needed to act to curb the health crisis. He lifted the ban on the needle exchange program, and since April 2015, over ninety-seven thousand needles have been distributed and returned and the number of people testing for HIV in the following months decreased drastically.[16]

CHAPTER SEVEN

Blazing a New Trail

• • • • • • • • • • • • • •

I n May of 2016, Pence began campaigning for reelection as Indiana's governor. As the race heated up against Democrat John Gregg, the *Indianapolis Star* printed an article that showed a large percentage of people didn't think Pence should be reelected.[1] His approval ratings had dropped after he signed the Religious Freedom Restoration Act, and he was struggling to regain ground. It was going to be a hard fight to maintain a his seat as governor.

While Pence was in the fight for a second term as governor, businessman Donald Trump was scouring the Republican ranks for a solid running mate in his 2016 race for the White House. After Trump won the Republican nomination over seventeen other contenders, including Ted Cruz, Jeb Bush, Marco Rubio, Rand Paul, and Ben Carson, he talked with numerous potential running mates before meeting with Pence at the governor's mansion in early July.

For the primaries of the Republican presidential nomination, Pence actually came out in support of Ted Cruz, a Texas senator who did well in the primaries initially, but Pence also managed to throw some praise in Trump's direction, which was an unusual tactic after endorsing a different candidate. While Pence was the final choice for vice presidential running mate, he was certainly not the only one considered for the job. Among those in the running were Newt Gingrich, a Republican politician who campaigned for the presidential nomination in 2012, and Chris Christie, the New Jersey governor. On July 14, 2016, Trump officially announced that he had chosen Mike Pence as his vice presidential running mate. That gave Pence mere hours to officially withdraw his name from Indiana's gubernatorial race, as the deadline for such action was at noon on July 15.[2]

The Conservative and the Rebel

The differences between Trump and Pence were noticeable. Pence was calm and quiet compared to Trump's abrasive, look-at-me demeanor. Seemingly opposite on paper, the two were both willing to go against the norm in the face of criticism and harsh opposition. Trump was a businessman and billionaire while Pence was a career politician and was never worth much more than $200,000 in his best years.[3] Trump had been married three times and didn't hide his appreciation and desire for the opposite sex. Pence had married in his mid-twenties and remained faithful to his wife, famously declaring that he wouldn't dine alone with a woman even for business out of respect for his wife and his marriage.[4]

Trump prided himself on saying whatever was on his mind while Pence was more guarded, choosing his words carefully and seemingly more willing to engage with and listen to other opinions.

The outward differences between the two men actually helped balance them out as a team. Those within Republican circles felt that Trump had made the right choice by picking Pence as his running mate. Pence's tempered personality helped to smooth the rough edges of Trump's personality, but only to a degree. And their

Donald Trump announced Pence as his running mate on July 14, 2016. Trump seriously considered several candidates to run on the vice presidential ticket, but he ultimately chose Pence.

political views, while perhaps not completely aligned either, seemed to mesh well. Where they might not agree, during the campaign Pence made sure to show deference to Trump and always expressed the utmost respect for him as a person and future leader of the country.

Pence offered solid political credentials to Trump's campaign. While signing the Religious Freedom Restoration Act caused Pence considerable backlash, he was a consistent, conservative politician who knew his way around the world of politics. For all his bravado, this was an area in which Trump was lacking, making Pence an invaluable part of the team he was building. Even though none of the bills Pence sponsored as a congressman came into law, Pence had extensive experience crafting, reading, and contributing to legislative issues.

In late July, Pence hit the campaign trail with Trump. They went to Virginia and North Carolina first, addressing people at a town hall. Pence made sure to allow Trump to take the main spotlight as he occasionally jumped in to show people how Trump would focus on the needs of the American people. He gave a few nods to their conservative agenda—issues like pro-life support—and Trump made sure to brag about his positive rating at the polls. Pence approached the crowd with a smooth voice and friendly smile, sometimes having to make up for Trump's more aggressive, and sometimes offensive, nature.

In their first interview together with Leslie Stahl on *60 Minutes*, Pence and Trump appeared mostly comfortable and relaxed with each other, though Trump certainly dominated the conversation. Early on in

On the campaign trail, Pence offered a quiet but solid figure in contrast to Trump's energetic and sometimes abrasive persona.

the interview, Pence noted that he was eager to stand beside Trump because he exhibited tough American strength that Pence believed was lacking during the Obama administration. When Stahl brought up some of the recent events happening around the world, such as a military coup in Turkey and a terrorist bombing in France, Trump spoke about the necessity of making a strong stand against any enemies of the United States. After he declared his intentions to go to war with ISIS, Stahl tried to unearth what Trump meant exactly. Pence jumped in and calmly noted that Trump's leadership and ability to take decisive action was exactly what the country needed without directly answering her question.[5]

When they moved on to discuss why Trump chose Pence, Stahl pointed out some of their policy differences. Pence voted for the War in Iraq when Trump had opposed it. Pence leaned toward traditional establishment where Trump didn't. And Pence spoke out against negative campaigning while Trump openly called his Democratic opponent Hillary Clinton a liar and a crook. When she pointed out this last difference, Stahl asked Pence if he would be able to tell Trump when he was out of line. Ever the politician, Pence didn't address the question directly but rather told Stahl that he and Trump shared the same vision, indicating that despite their different styles, they were very much on the same page. Only after Trump acknowledged that he would appreciate honest feedback from Pence did Pence agree that he would have no hesitation addressing issues candidly with the presidential hopeful.[6]

Debates and Drama

As he moved on to the vice presidential debate with Democrat Tim Kaine, Pence was able to express the vision he shared with Trump. Both men often danced around questions the moderator asked and interrupted each other a great deal, with Kaine interrupting Pence a whopping seventy times, nearly double the amount of time Pence interrupted him.[7] They covered topics such as health care, foreign policy, taxes, policing, and the way their respective running mates were handling the campaign.

When the issue of Trump's personal taxes arose, Kaine wanted to know if Pence believed Trump should release his tax returns to the public. The moderator followed

Tim Kaine

Like Mike Pence, Tim Kaine embraced a deeply personal faith that guided his principles and shaped his political outlook. He was a Virginia senator who had followed a similar trajectory as Pence in that he practiced law before pursuing politics and was elected as mayor of Richmond, Virginia, in 1998. While Pence and Kaine supported different parties, they both considered themselves to be old-fashioned in some ways. Interestingly enough, Kaine and Pence agree on one hot-topic issue, they both are personally against abortion, but their outlook on where the government should get involved differs greatly. Kaine noted that his personal beliefs don't change his opinion that a woman has the right to choose, saying that with much greater issues to worry about, the government doesn't "need to make people's reproductive decisions for them."[8]

up by rephrasing a question she seemed to feel Pence hadn't answered regarding Trump's boast that he paid as little as possible in taxes by knowing the tax laws so well. The defense Pence came back with was that Trump was a businessman, not a politician. That response clearly didn't satisfy Kaine, as he declared that Trump was dishonoring the American way by not contributing his fair share through taxes to teachers, military, and other important public services.[9] As the discussion heated up, the moderator finally had to step in to move to two men forward to other topics.

The vice presidential debate against Tim Kaine was sometimes strained, with both men interrupting each other many times.

• • • • • • • • • • • • • • • • • • • •

Over the course of the debate, both Pence and Kaine talked about times when their rivals had crossed lines and engaged in negative tactics on the campaign trail. For example, Kaine discussed how Trump had angered numerous groups of people with derogatory, dismissive comments about minorities, Muslims, and women. He pointed out that he felt it was uncouth and exemplified poor leadership skills and that good behavior should start from the top. Pence responded by pointing out how Clinton had called those who supported Trump a

Stronger Together

Hilary Clinton's slogan for her 2016 campaign was officially "Stronger Together," intended to symbolize the unity and strength that the Democrat team was fighting so hard to obtain. One of the earlier versions of Clinton's slogan was "I'm With Her," but that didn't seem to catch on or have the same positive effect on people that her newer slogan did. The "Stronger Together" slogan embraced inclusiveness and implied that the power of America lay with the people if they would just unite behind a good leader. Donald Trump's slogan for the 2016 campaign was "Make America Great Again," implying that he was going to work hard to lift the country back up to the great space it once occupied. It seemed to resonate well with people who were fed up with politicians who knew how to speak well but often failed to deliver on their promises. His slogan promised to bring the country back to better times.

"basket of deplorables" and Kaine quickly noted that she had apologized for her comment.[10]

Pence talked about how Clinton's time as secretary of state had weakened the country's foreign policy. He asserted that he and Trump had a plan to rebuild a strong foreign policy and that a lack of leadership during Obama's administration led to the country being less safe than ever before. He pointed out that Obamacare would be repealed, not revised as Clinton and Kaine aimed to do, and that he and Trump would get the economy

Pence took to the stage on election night after the official announcement came that Donald Trump had won the presidency.

• • • • • • • • • • • • • • • • • • • •

moving again by making sure jobs stayed in America and taxes were lowered across the board. Kaine rebutted by focusing on how he and Clinton had a plan to research clean energy jobs, raise the minimum wage, and provide tuition-free college to families that qualified.

As the election drew near, tapes were leaked to the press that revealed Trump in 2005 talking about how he could grope women—and had indeed done so— because he was powerful and famous. Though he noted that he was personally offended and disappointed in the tapes, Pence came to Trump's defense by saying that the presidential candidate was apologetic for his comments and deserved the right to a second chance. He also added that the incident happened long ago and that the American people were more concerned about other issues, hinting that the press was merely trying to find

> "The American people have spoken and the American people have elected their new champion."

reasons to discredit Trump. Still willing to stand behind Trump 100 percent, Pence had this to say: "People are struggling in this economy to make ends meet and they see in Hillary Clinton someone who wants to continue all the same failed policies that have weakened America's place in the world and stifled our economy."[11] While it did cause a hiccup in the campaign, the leaked tapes soon seemed to get shuffled to the backburner.

On November 9, the official announcement came: Donald Trump had won the 2016 presidential election and would become the next president of the United States. It came as a shock to many, but it was a closer race than the months leading up to the campaign had suggested. Pence addressed the American people from their Trump headquarters, giving a few short remarks to lead the way into the next chapter of his life:

> This is a historic night. The American people have spoken and the American people have elected their new champion. America has elected a new president and it's almost hard for me to express the honor that I and my family feel that we will have the privilege to serve as the Vice President of the United States. I come

to this moment deeply humbled, grateful to God for his amazing grace, grateful to my family: my wonderful wife Karen, our son Michael, and his fiancee Sarah, our daughter Audrey far away, and our daughter Charlotte. I could not be here without them and I'm deeply grateful to the American people for placing their confidence in this team and giving us this opportunity to serve. And I'm mostly grateful to the president elect whose leadership and vision will make America great again.[12]

Whether people were ready or not, Trump and Pence were headed to the White House.

CHAPTER EIGHT

White House Bound

. . . .

In the days that followed Trump's presidential win in the 2016 election, many people were celebrating, but many more were so upset that they gathered to protest. On November 11, thousands of protesters marched on downtown Portland, Denver, New York, Los Angeles, and San Francisco, to name a few cities. Dozens were arrested when some protestors got aggressive with police. When the march moved onto the freeway in Denver, Interstate 25 had to be shut down briefly. The chants and slogans among the groups ranged from "We reject the president-elect" to "Not My President" to "Make America Safe for All."[1] For a short period of time there was even an attempt to commission a recount of the election votes due to the belief that fraud had occurred. One of the independent candidates in the presidential election, Jill Stein, who had received only a very minor percentage of the vote, tried to raise funds to prompt the recount, but the move didn't make a difference. Donald Trump would become the next president, despite the disappointment of many.

In the months that followed her defeat, Hillary Clinton began working on a memoir that examined the 2016 campaign and those responsible for her downfall. It was titled *What Happened* and was published in late 2017. Clinton felt that there were numerous reasons she lost, but in the book she blamed everyone from Bernie Sanders to Russian president Vladimir Putin to former FBI director James Comey.[2] In a daytime television interview that took place just after her book came out, Clinton pinpointed the former FBI director as the nail in her coffin. In the days leading up to the presidential election, Comey chose to reopen an investigation into emails that Clinton sent during her time as secretary of state—the same emails that Pence declared in his vice presidential debate were illegal and wrong and would have landed a regular citizen in jail.[3]

Early Days in Office

As Clinton was dealing with her disappointment, Trump and Pence were preparing for Inauguration Day. January 20, 2017, came quickly for the Trump-Pence Team. It was a chilly winter morning, and Pence took some time to reflect and pray before officially beginning Inauguration Day. He wore a crisp dark suit and black coat, accented by a bright blue tie. A cold drizzle came off and on throughout the morning as thousands of people crowded in front of the US Capitol to watch the historic moment. From Pence's point of view, standing behind Trump's right shoulder, he could see down the west side

Pence requested that he be sworn into office with a Bible once owned by Ronald Reagan, one of his political idols.

• • • • • • • • • • • • • • • • • • • •

of the Capitol and all the way down the National Mall to the towering Washington Monument.

When it came time for Pence to step up to the podium and be sworn in, he put his hand on a Bible that had belonged to Ronald Reagan, one of his political idols, and took the oath administered by Supreme Court justice Clarence Thomas. His wife held the Bible and gazed at him with solemn pride while his children stood close by. After he completed the oath, Pence stepped back and looked on with pride as his running mate was sworn in as the forty-fifth president of the United States.

One of the first duties Trump gave Pence was to be in charge of investigating the illegal voting Trump claimed took place in the election. Trump declared that multiple registrations had taken place. He noted that illegal immigrants and even dead people had cast votes, indicating fraud at worst and an imperfect system at best.[4] Thus, Pence was given charge to delve deeper into the matter. While other experts and politicians agreed that a small amount of election fraud can and does occur, it isn't usually enough to warrant a full-scale investigation. Pence took the assignment seriously and began examining potential cracks in the voting system, but the commission was disbanded a short time later before any real progress was made.

A Chance for Promotion

If the president were unable to perform the duties of office, usually because of resignation or death, the vice president would take over the position. If both the president and vice president were removed at the same time for some reason, the Speaker of the House would take over. Beyond the Speaker of the House, a long list of succession exists but has never had to be implemented. Since the inception of the presidency of the United States, eight presidents have died—and four of these have been by assassination—in which case their vice president took over. Richard Nixon is the only president in US history who has resigned. Two presidents were impeached—Andrew Johnson and Bill Clinton—but they were later acquitted and didn't leave their presidency.

Just a week after the inauguration, Pence attended a March for Life event. His appearance made him the highest-elected official to ever attend a March for Life event to date, but Pence's long-time pro-life stance made it an honor for him to attend. The Supreme Court ruled to legalize abortion in the 1973 case of *Roe v. Wade*, but ever since that ruling, a battle has ensued between those fighting for pro-life rights and pro-choice rights. Around the anniversary of the court's January ruling, a March for Life event has happened every year since 1974. Women and men lined the street to listen to Pence deliver a short speech. He proudly declared that he and President Trump were dedicated to promoting a culture of life during their time in office. They were working to fight for the rights of all human life by defunding Planned Parenthood and stopping taxpayer dollars from going toward abortions.[5]

Despite being a powerful public figure, the only real constitutional responsibility of the vice president is to oversee the Senate and cast a vote in case of a tie (a duty some vice presidents didn't perform at all during their term). John Adams, the country's first vice president, thought that the role was "the most insignificant office that ever the invention of man contrived."[6] While he might have seen the duties of second-in-command as less than exciting, Adams went on to become the second president of the United States. Beyond the duty to cast a tiebreaking vote, the vice president often leads special commissions, meets with political leaders, and attends ceremonial functions.

Pence had always been clear about his stance on abortion. Just one week after the Inauguration, he became the highest elected official to ever attend a March for Life event.

Even though the job of vice president does not come with many truly heavy responsibilities, it does come with a number of perks and interesting benefits. For one, the vice president gets his own plane, Air Force Two. He is able to take the plane anywhere in the world and generally uses it for visits to other states or countries. The vice president is also provided with a residence that is just minutes from the White House. The home boasts thirty-three rooms and is on the grounds of the U.S. Naval Observatory. He also has an office in the West Wing of the White House, just down the hall from the

Air Force Two

Air Force Two is a Boeing C-32 and transports the vice president of the United States. Other aircraft have also served as the official transportation for the vice president over the years, but the current choice is the Boeing C-32, which is a modified Boeing 737. Air Force Two has four main sections. Some of the features include a communications center; a fully enclosed stateroom with a private changing room, entertainment system, and lavatory; a conference and staff facility; a galley; and numerous areas that host business class seats.[7] It is a custom for the outgoing vice president to pick up the incoming vice president and his family in Air Force Two, so on January 9, 2017, former vice president Joe Biden sent his aircraft to pick up Pence and his wife and bring them from Indiana to Washington, DC.

Oval Office, and has up to eighty aides available to help with his projects.[8]

Along with the various duties he carried as vice president, Pence worked to make a difference in smaller ways within local communities. When a Jewish cemetery was vandalized in February 2017 in St. Louis, Missouri, Pence visited the site and helped clean it up alongside Missouri governor Eric Greitens and members of the community. He gave a short talk before the cleanup began about how hatred and prejudice have no place among America's most cherished values.[9]

Pence made time to visit a Jewish cemetery in St. Louis in February 2017 after it was vandalized. After speaking out against hatred and prejudice, he rolled up his sleeves and helped clean up the cemetery.

In March 2017, the Republicans in the House of Representatives rolled out their new healthcare plan, which they hoped would gain enough traction to replace the Affordable Care Act (also known as Obamacare).[10] The proposed bill would no longer force people to buy insurance or require larger employers to offer coverage to full-time employees. The Republicans proposed keeping some parts of Obamacare but changing and dropping other parts. The House was deeply divided about the effectiveness of Obamacare, but they were also unsure about the new plan. When the plan was pulled from the House floor, Pence tried to convince businesses that their efforts to repeal and replace the current health care system would continue.

Some vice presidents were never needed to serve as president of the Senate, but after just a year in office Pence had acted as tiebreaker eight times. Pence cast the tiebreaking vote for Planned Parenthood to be denied funds on a state-by-state basis; he voted to nominate Betsy DeVos as secretary of education; and he also voted to nominate Kansas governor Sam Brownback as ambassador-at-large for international religious freedom.[11] These were just three of the issues in which Pence was able to act as the tiebreaker within the Senate.

Although Pence was naturally overshadowed by the president—not only because of his role but also because of his calmer nature—he was actually doing better in the polls than Trump soon after taking office. In a poll taken by *USA Today* and Suffolk University, the vice president had 47 percent of the population expressing a "generally favorable impression" of him, which put him ahead of most politicians in Washington, including Trump and Clinton.[12]

Tours of Public Service

In late April of 2017, Pence made a trip overseas to visit a number of countries in the Pacific region. During a stop in Japan he spoke to political leaders about trade agreements. President Trump had expressed concern for the United States with regards to unbalanced trade that was taking place with Japan and China. He had recently removed the United States from the Trans-Pacific Partnership trade and wanted Pence to sit down with the prime minister of Japan to discuss ways to level the playing field and work out a deal that would be more beneficial for the United States.

Pence also visited South Korea, Indonesia, Australia, and Hawaii on his tour. During his time in South Korea, Pence especially focused on the issues facing the country, which shares a border with the hostile country of North Korea. Tensions were high because North Korea's leader, Kim Jong-un, was unpredictable and had been threatening to unleash nuclear terror. If he did act on his threats, it could be devastating for South Korea but also could create a major crisis for world leaders. After North Korea tested a ballistic missile just two and a half weeks before Pence's arrival to the Pacific region, President Trump made it clear that he would respond aggressively if Kim Jong-un did carry out an attack.[13]

In June 2017, Pence made a visit to NASA, touring the facility and giving a speech to the newest NASA trainees. While over eighteen thousand people applied for the

NASA training program, a mere twelve made it through to completion and were able to call themselves astronauts. As he addressed the graduates and their families, Pence was clearly very proud of their accomplishments. He assured them that the country would stand behind them as they pushed into new territory and attained new heights in space exploration.

As always, Pence mentioned the president and his hopes for the graduates and left them with this message:

> Under the leadership of President Donald Trump, the United States will usher in a new era of space exploration that will benefit every facet of our national life. It will strengthen our national security and the safety of the American people. It will strengthen our economy, as we unlock new opportunities and new sources of prosperity. It will strengthen education in inspiring a rising generation of Americans to study science, technology, engineering, and math. And more than anything else, as the President believes with deep conviction, we'll strengthen the American spirit—as once again, we reach out our hands to touch the heavens and raise our heads to gaze with wonder at the stars and the heroes that have the courage to explore them.[14]

On September 20, 2017, a devastating hurricane touched down in Puerto Rico. The storm produced winds that reached 155 miles per hour, which made it barely under a Category 5 hurricane and killed the power to the entire island. In some

> "We'll strengthen the American spirit—as once again, we reach out our hands to touch the heavens."

towns, most buildings were destroyed and massive flooding ensued after the main storm had passed. Four days after the storm hit, Pence spoke with Puerto Rico's representative in the House of Representatives, Jenniffer González-Colón, but it took an additional two days for President Trump to hold a meeting in the Situation Room to discuss official aid the government would provide to Puerto Rico. Soon, a hospital ship, USNS *Comfort*, was on the way, along with additional cargo aircraft with water, food, and other supplies.[15]

Many were critical of how long it took for President Trump to respond with aid relief for the island, especially considering that the storm was even worse than ones like Hurricane Harvey in Houston and Hurricane Irma in Florida, both of which occurred within two months of the disaster in Puerto Rico. The Federal Emergency Management Agency (FEMA) was deployed to help after each of the three storms, but FEMA's presence in Puerto Rico was less than in Houston and Florida, and it took longer to arrive.[16] Pence went to visit the devastated island during the first week of October and did what he could to reassure the people there that they would do all they could to help with the crisis. He spoke with Virgin Islands governor Kenneth Mapp, who noted that the government was working with them and providing all their requests. Pence also toured the capital of Puerto Rico, San Juan, and met with people, talking to them and listening to their frustrations and concerns.[17]

Just after his visit to Puerto Rico, Pence and his wife were scheduled to attend an NFL game in Indianapolis between the Indianapolis Colts and San Francisco 49ers.

Pence visited Puerto Rico in October 2017, soon after the island was hit by a massive hurricane. He offered reassurance that the United States would do its part to help during the time of crisis.

While some of the NFL players knelt during the National Anthem, the Pences stood proudly with their hands over their hearts. Just after the song was finished, they left the game and Pence tweeted the following message: "President Trump and I will not dignify any event that disrespects our soldiers, our Flag, or our National Anthem. While everyone is entitled to their own opinion, I don't think it's too much to ask NFL players to respect the flag and our national anthem." The controversy over kneeling during the National Anthem had been going on for weeks. Many of the NFL players participating in the silent protest expressed their concerns for the racism and social injustices happening around the country and cited that as their reason for kneeling, rather than an intention to disrespect the military. But many, including Trump and Pence, saw it as a negative move to create division and create conflict.

In the first year of his vice presidency, Pence traveled to numerous countries, spoke at multiple functions, made countless appearances, and presided over the Senate. As the first year came to a close, new challenges came and old ones were resolved. In his unique role, Pence was striving to create a better future for the United States.

CHAPTER NINE

No Rest for the Weary

. . . .

As Pence continued to attend to his duties as vice president, his wife, Karen, focused her attention on using art therapy as a way to help those with physical and mental illnesses. As a former elementary school teacher and artist, Karen has had a passion for art therapy for years. She stated that many people misunderstand art therapy. "It is not arts and crafts," she said. "It is not therapeutic art. For art therapy, you have to have the art and the client and the therapist, the trained therapist who has a clinical psychology background, who is somebody who can lead the client through the process."[1] During their numerous trips, Karen has met with art therapists and visited many art therapy programs. She even brought 100 pounds (45 kilograms) of clay to an art therapy program in Puerto Rico after Hurricane Maria.

A Visit to Israel

After ringing in the New Year, Pence lost some of his top aides. Though a usually high number of aides seemed to leave the White House under the Trump administration, the work continued. In the later part of January, Pence made a trip to the Middle East. This came soon after President Trump announced that the United States would be moving the American Embassy in Israel from Tel Aviv to Jerusalem.[2] This was a promise Trump made during his presidential campaign but one that he knew would cause debate and controversy when he announced it at the end of the year in 2017.

The conflict between Israel and Palestine has been going on for centuries and is mainly over land ownership. While Israel is a country, the state of Palestine exists within the space bordering Israel and Egypt. Israel is the only Jewish country in the region surrounded by Muslim countries. Both Israelis and Palestinians view Jerusalem as a most sacred land. By moving the American Embassy to Jerusalem, the United States would be sending the message that it is more on the side of the Israelis in the conflict between the two territories.[3] Pence spoke at the Israeli parliament during his trip but did not meet with the Palestinians, further advancing this theory. Both Presidents Bill Clinton and George W. Bush declared their intentions to move the embassy, but it never happened.[4]

Olympic Controversies

As February rolled around, Pence prepared to head to the Winter Olympics in PyeongChang, South Korea. Seated

Pence visited Israel in January 2018, soon after President Trump announced that the US Embassy would move from Tel Aviv to Jerusalem.

School Safety

After yet another school shooting took place in Parkland, Florida, in February 2018, Pence spoke about the urgent need to make schools safer for young people across the country. He focused on the importance of "taking a renewed look at giving law enforcement and local authorities the tools they need to deal with dangerous mental illness."[5] While some members of Congress and the media called for gun control reforms in the wake of the shooting, Pence didn't focus on that issue during his speech, which brought criticism against the Trump administration from those who feel that gun reform laws are absolutely necessary. Rather, he encouraged people to pray so the country could come together and find the best solutions to an increasing problem.

just behind Pence and his wife at the opening ceremonies was the sister of North Korea's dictator, Kim Jong-un. No introduction or exchange, formal or informal, took place between Pence and the dictator's sister, but South Korea's president, Moon Jae-in, welcomed her warmly. President Moon Jae-in expressed that he hoped the Olympics would be a time to bring people together and set aside differences, if only temporarily.

Some felt that Pence's unwillingness to overlook differences and be polite or extend any courtesy to the North Korean government was too rigid considering the context. Yet Pence was unapologetic. He had met

The Pences attended opening ceremonies for the 2018 Winter Olympics in PyeongChang, South Korea. Seated close by was the sister of North Korea's dictator, Kim Jong-un. No words or exchange took place between the parties.

> **"[T]he United States of America doesn't stand with murderous dictatorships, we stand up to murderous dictatorships."**

with North Koreans who had risked their lives to escape the country during his time at the Olympics, and he found their stories harrowing.[6] He spoke soon after at the Conservative Political Action Conference and had these words to share regarding his feelings toward North Korea:

> The sister of Kim Jong Un is a central pillar of the most tyrannical and oppressive regime on the planet, an evil family clique that brutalizes, subjugates, starves and imprisons its 25 million people. For all those in the media who think I should have stood and cheered with the North Koreans, I say: the United States of America doesn't stand with murderous dictatorships, we stand up to murderous dictatorships.[7]

Another controversy that was highlighted at the Winter Olympics but started in the weeks leading up to it was when twenty-eight-year-old Adam Rippon, a figure skater on the US Olympic Team, said he was disappointed that Vice President Pence was the head of the US delegation for the Winter Games. Rippon, an openly gay man, threw a spotlight on some of the views that Pence embraced regarding LGBTQ rights and also proclaimed that he would have nothing to say to Pence if they ever met.[8] Some news outlets claimed that Pence had reached out to Rippon, and Rippon refused his phone call. While it did cause a stir for a short time, Pence's press secretary issued a statement expressing Pence's

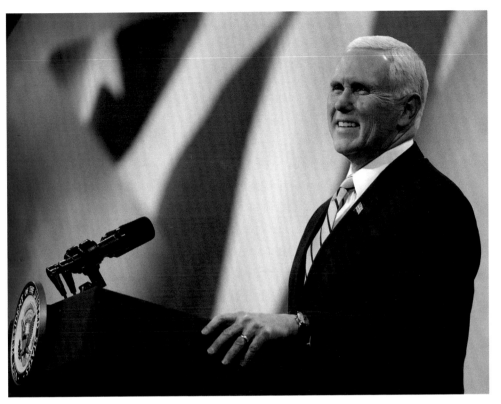

Pence has enjoyed a long career pursuing his passion for public service. As congressman, governor, and vice president, he has helped shape the political landscape.

● ●

wholehearted support for all US Olympic athletes and that Rippon's belief that Pence supported gay conversion therapy was "completely false."[9]

His long career in politics has allowed Pence to live his passion for public service. It has given him the opportunity to connect with all types of people, listening, sharing, and contributing to shaping the future through legislation and law reform. Pence aimed to stand by his principles of conservativism and faith even when it has made him unpopular and criticized. Pence's next move is unclear. While President Trump endured low approval ratings in the polls in his first year in office, it is possible that he will run for a second term.[10] Does Pence have ambitions to lead the country? Regardless of his future course, Pence will likely continue to serve the American people.

Mike Pence has spent a lifetime dedicated to advancing his political goals and ideologies. He is a man who holds tightly to his faith, his family, and his country. For all the naysayers who criticize his views there are others who stand behind him in support and appreciation. Regardless, Pence has enjoyed a prosperous, though sometimes rocky, career in a field he loves.

Chronology

1959 Mike Pence is born in Columbus, Indiana, on June 7.

1977 Takes first place in the American Legion's Indiana Oratorical Contest.

1981 Graduates from Hanover College with a BA in history.

1983 Meets Karen Batten at a mass service and they begin dating.

1984 Marries Karen on June 8.

1986 Graduates from Indiana University's Robert H. McKinney's School of Law and begins his career as an attorney in private practice.

1988 Runs for Congress on the Republican ticket against Democrat Phil Sharp and loses.

1990 Runs for Congress a second time and loses to Phil Sharp again.

1991 Becomes president of the Indiana Policy Review Foundation.

1992 Begins hosting a radio program called *The Mike Pence Show*.

2000 Runs for Congress a third time and wins a seat in the House of Representatives, a position he would maintain for a total of six terms.

2001 Votes against the No Child Left Behind Act proposed by President George W. Bush.

2002 Votes against the Medicare prescription drug expansion bill.

2006 Runs for leader of the Republican Party in the House of Representatives but loses to John Boehner.

2008 Pence votes against the Wall Street bailout proposition (TARP).

2008 *Esquire* names Pence one of the top ten best members of Congress.

2009 Elected to one of the highest ranking positions in the Republican Party as Republican Conference chairman.

2013 Becomes governor of Indiana on January 14.

2014 After a State of the State address in which Pence argued that the Common Core Initiative in education should be repealed, Indiana became the first state to do so.

2015 Signs the Religious Freedom Restoration Act (RFRA) into law on March 26 and receives harsh criticism. Due to the backlash, Pence revised—but did not repeal—RFRA to protect anyone from possible discrimination.

2016 On June 14, Donald Trump announces that Pence will be his vice presidential running mate in the 2016 presidential race and Pence removes himself from the race for the Indiana governor's seat the next day; Pence debates Democratic vice presidential candidate Tim Kaine on October 4;

on November 9, Trump is declared winner of the presidential race.

2017 Donald Trump and Mike Pence are sworn in as president and vice president of the United States of America on January 20. Pence speaks at a March for Life event in Washington, DC, on January 27. Independent Women's Forum honors Pence with the Working for Women Award in March. Pence gives a commencement speech at the US Naval Academy in Maryland in May. In October, Pence and his wife visit the island of Puerto Rico after it was ravaged by Hurricane Maria. On November 16, Pence receives the Tax Foundation's Distinguished Service Award for his work in tax reform and tax policy. On November 28, Pence receives the 2017 Herman Kahn Award from the Hudson Institute for being a public servant who exhibits foresight and commitment to keeping the country safe.

2018 Travels to the Middle East and addresses the Israeli parliament about moving the American Embassy from Tel Aviv to Jerusalem on January 22. On January 24, breaks a tie in the Senate for the eighth time since taking office as vice president. Attends the Opening Ceremonies for the Winter Olympic Games on February 9. Speaks about the urgent need to make schools safer after a teenager opened fire on a high school in Parkland, Florida, on February 17.

Chapter Notes

Chapter 1: Born in a Sleepy Indiana Town

1. Zack Peterson, "Vice President's Mother Discusses Young Mike Pence and Her First Time in Chattanooga" *Times Free Press*, May 20, 2017, http://www.timesfreepress.com/news/local/story/2017/may/20/vice-president-pences-mother-discusses-very-t/429144/.

2. Sinead O'Shea and Mitch Smith, "Mike Pence's 1980s Visit to His Grandfather's Home" *Irish Times*, March 17, 2017, https://www.irishtimes.com/life-and-style/people/mike-pence-s-1980s-visit-to-his-grandfather-s-home-1.3014503.

3. Susan Stamberg, "Columbus, Indiana: A Midwestern Mecca of Architecture," National Public Radio, July 31, 2012, https://www.npr.org/2012/08/04/157675872/columbus-ind-a-midwestern-mecca-of-architecture.

4. Maureen Groppe, "Vice President Mike Pence Learned from His Father the Lingering Burdens Veterans Bear," *IndyStar*, November 11, 2017, https://www.indystar.com/story/news/politics/2017/11/11/vice-president-mike-pence-learned-his-father-lingering-burdens-veterans-bear/855145001/.

5. Jonathan Mahler and Dirk Johnson, "Mike Pence's Journey: Catholic Democrat to Evangelical

Republican," *New York Times*, July 20, 2016, https://
www.nytimes.com/2016/07/21/us/politics/mike-
pence-religion.html.

6. Harry McCawley, "The Mike Pence Story: From a
Youth in Columbus to Candidate for Vice President,"
Republic, January 13, 2013, http://www.therepublic.
com/2016/07/14/the-mike-pence-story-from-a-
youth-in-columbus-to-candidate-for-vice-president/#.
Wlek9z2XxBk.email.

7. Ibid.

8. Peterson.

9. McCawley.

10. Heather Cherone, "Mike Pence's South Side Roots:
I Owe A Debt of Gratitude to Chicago," *DNAinfo*,
January 20, 2016, https://www.dnainfo.com/
chicago/20170120/englewood/mike-pence-chicago-
childhood-immigrant-grandparents-parents-uncle-
police-cop.

11. O'Shea and Smith.

12. Ibid.

13. "1959 History/Videos," http://
www.1959bhsmustangs.com/1959historicalevents.
htm.

14. Ryan Lovelace, "Mike Pence Touts Admiration for
JFK in Ohio," *Washington Examiner*, October 7, 2016,
http://www.washingtonexaminer.com/mike-pence-
touts-admiration-for-jfk-in-ohio/article/2603912.

Chapter 2: Faith, Marriage, and Future

1. McKay Coppins, "God's Plan for Mike Pence: Will the Vice President—and the Religious Right—Be Rewarded for Their Embrace of Donald Trump?" *Atlantic*, Jan/Feb 2018, https://www.theatlantic.com/magazine/archive/2018/01/gods-plan-for-mike-pence/546569/?utm_source=atltw.

2. Jeremy Berke, "Here Are All the Most Outrageous Things Mike Pence's Brother Said About Him," *Business Insider*, October 18, 2017, http://www.businessinsider.com/mike-pence-brother-greg-names-2017-10.

3. Jonathan Mahler and Dirk Johnson, "Mike Pence's Journey: Catholic Democrat to Evangelical Republican," *New York Times*, July 20, 2016, https://www.nytimes.com/2016/07/21/us/politics/mike-pence-religion.html.

4. Frank Freidel and Hug Sidey, "The Presidents of the United States of America," Whitehouse.gov, https://www.whitehouse.gov/about-the-white-house/presidents/ronald-reagan.

5. Mahler and Johnson.

6. Shari Rudavsky, "Karen Pence Is Right at Home," *Indy Star*, December 12, 2013, https://www.indystar.com/story/life/2013/12/12/karen-pence-is-right-at-home/3997289/.

7. Ibid.

8. Melissa Langsam Braunstein, "Second Lady Karen Pence Opens Up About Her Struggles With Infertility," *Federalist*, April 25, 2017, http://

thefederalist.com/2017/04/25/second-lady-karen-pence-opens-struggles-infertility/.

9. Ibid.

10. Ibid.

11. Martin Pritikin, "Law School Requirements," Concord Law School, https://www.concordlawschool.edu/student-life/law-school-requirements.

12. Michael Cavna, "Here Are the Cartoons Mike Pence Drew While in Law School," *Washington Post*, August 25, 2016, https://www.washingtonpost.com/news/comic-riffs/wp/2016/08/25/here-are-the-cartoons-mike-pence-drew-while-in-law-school/?utm_term=.60346bd203f3.

13. Debra Cassens Weiss, "Trump's VP Pick Practiced Law at a Small Firm: He Wouldn't Wish Law School 'on a Dog I Didn't Like,'" *ABA Journal*, July 18, 2016, http://www.abajournal.com/news/article/trumps_vp_pick_practiced_law_at_a_small_firm_he_wouldnt_wish_law_school_on.

Chapter 3: Plunge into the Political Pool

1. Harry McCawley, "The Mike Pence Story: From a Youth in Columbus to Vice President of the United States," *Republic*, January 13, 2013, http://www.therepublic.com/2016/07/14/the-mike-pence-story-from-a-youth-in-columbus-to-candidate-for-vice-president.

2. Ibid.

3. "House of Representatives," Encyclopedia Britannica, https://www.britannica.com/topic/House-of-Representatives-United-States-government.

4. Rosalind S. Helderman, Tom Hamburger, and Alice Crites, "Mike Pence Used Campaign Funds to Pay His Mortgage—and It Cost Him an Election," *Washington Post*, July 15, 2016, https://www.washingtonpost.com/politics/mike-pence-used-campaign-funds-to-pay-his-mortgage--and-it-cost-him-an-election/2016/07/15/90858964-49ed-11e6-bdb9-701687974517_story.html?utm_term=.7951a360c4a2.

5. John Schorg, "Pence Hopes to Overcome Outsider Role," *Republic*, September 25, 1988, https://www.newspapers.com/clip/15673906/mike_pence_1988/.

6. S. Helderman, Hamburger, and Crites.

7. Ibid.

8. Ibid.

9. Mike Pence, "Confessions of a Negative Campaigner," Indiana Policy Review Foundation, October 1991.

10. Ibid.

Chapter 4: The Developing Communicator

1. Matt Viser, "How Mike Pence Found His Footing," *Boston Globe*, July 20, 2016, https://www.bostonglobe.com/news/nation/2016/07/19/for-mike-pence-political-career-was-launched-when-his-talk-radio-show-took-off/KUkYKbl77vJ6yntVBBUM0L/story.html.

2. Ibid.

3. Ibid.

4. Ibid.

5. Elaine Sciolino, "Air Force Chief Has Harsh Words for Pilot Facing Adultery Charges," *New York Times*, May 22, 1997, http://www.nytimes.com/books/97/12/14/home/052297airforce-pilot.html.

6. Ibid.

7. "Mike Pence – 2000 Trust," YouTube video, May 12, 2011, https://www.youtube.com/watch?v=bEycOlLkyXk.

8. *The Mike Pence Show*, YouTube video, January 10, 2017, https://www.youtube.com/watch?v=5pqb0GDu2mw.

9. "Mike Pence – 2000 – Straight Talk," YouTube video, September 16, 2008, https://www.youtube.com/watch?v=F9sIefTurj4.

10. "Mike Pence – 2000 Trust," YouTube video.

Chapter 5: Quiet Rebel

1. Catherine Garcia, "Mike Pence: I'm a Christian, a Conservative, and a Republican—in That Order," *The Week*, July 20, 2016, http://theweek.com/speedreads/637487/mike-pence-im-christian-conservative-republican--that-order.

2. "No Child Left Behind Act," Office of Superintendent of Public Instruction, State of Washington, http://www.k12.wa.us/esea/NCLB.aspx.

3. Ibid.

4. Times Editorial Board, "No Child Left Behind: How to End 'Teaching to the Test,'" *LA Times*, February 23, 2015, http://www.latimes.com/opinion/editorials/la-ed-testing-no-child-left-behind-20150223-story.html.

5. Bills and Resolutions in the United State Congress Sponsored by Mike Pence, Govtrack. us, https://www.govtrack.us/congress/bills/ browse?sponsor=400315#bill_type[]=3.

6. Philip Elliott, "Mike Pence Is No Ordinary Wingman," *Time*, December 26, 2016-January 2, 2017.

7. "Mike Pence's Long History Attacking Social Security & Medicare," National Committee to Preserve Social Security and Medicare, July 15, 2016, http://www. ncpssm.org/EntitledtoKnow/entryid/2221/mike-pence-s-long-history-attacking-social-security-medicare.

8. Bob Cusack, "When Newt and Pence Were on Opposite Sides," *The Hill*, July 13, 2016, http://thehill. com/policy/healthcare/287525-when-newt-and-pence-were-on-opposite-sides.

9. Elliott.

10. Bree Nordenson, "The Shield Bearer," *Columbia Journalism Review* (May/June 2007): 48–52.

11. David Stout, "The Wall Street Bailout Plan, Explained, *New York Times*, September 20, 2008, http://www.nytimes.com/2008/09/21/ business/21qanda.html.

12. Aaron P. Bernstein, "Trump VP Pick Mike Pence Wears His Opposition to 2008 Bank Bailouts with Pride," *NewsMaxFinance*, July 20, 2016, https://www. newsmax.com/finance/streettalk/donald-trump-mike-pence-bank-bailouts/2016/07/20/id/739631/.

13. Ibid.

Chapter 6: From Tax Cuts to Abortion Reform

1. Doug West, "Vice President Mike Pence: A Short Biography" (San Bernardino, CA, 2018), p. 14.

2. Sam Levine, "Mike Pence Once Thought a $7.25 Minimum Wage Was Too High," *Huffington Post*, July 16, 2016, https://www.huffingtonpost.com/entry/mike-pence-minimum-wage_us_578a8c22e4b0867123e190fd.

3. Maureen Hayden, "Indiana Lawmakers Override Pence on Local Measure," *Herald Bulletin*, June 12, 2013, http://www.heraldbulletin.com/archives/article_33e315ea-b1f5-5d7f-a99b-ffeb6231b818.html.

4. Steve Inskeep, "Former 'No Child Left Behind' Advocate Turns Critic," NPR, March 10, 2010, https://www.npr.org/templates/story/story.php?storyId=124209100.

5. West, p. 10.

6. "Stephanopoulos Grills Mike Pence Over LGBT discrim," YouTube video, December 5, 2016, https://www.youtube.com/watch?v=BAamBVTuaCU.

7. "Mike Pence on Abortion," Ballotpedia, https://ballotpedia.org/Mike_Pence_vice_presidential_campaign,_2016/Abortion, accessed February 11, 2018.

8. Mitch Smith and Erik Eckholm, "Federal Judge Blocks Indiana Abortion Law," *New York Times*, June 30, 2016, https://www.nytimes.com/2016/07/01/us/federal-judge-blocks-indiana-abortion-law.html?_r=0.

9. Ibid.

10. Dan Carden, "Pence Signs Law Expanding School Voucher Eligibility," *NWI Times*, May 9, 2013, http://www.nwitimes.com/news/local/govt-and-politics/pence-signs-law-expanding-school-voucher-eligibility/article_03841210-1ef2-5b47-ae7b-f7a0a1f4252f.html.

11. Ibid.

12. Kate Zernik, "Mike Pence's Record on Education Is One of Turmoil and Mixed Results," *New York Times*, July 19, 2016, https://www.nytimes.com/2016/07/20/us/politics/trump-vp-mike-pences-record-on-education.html.

13. West, p. 12.

14. Stephanie Wang, "Gov. Mike Pence Signs Bill to Allow Guns in School Parking Lots," *Indy Star*, March 26, 2014, https://www.indystar.com/story/news/education/2014/03/26/pence-signs-bill-allow-guns-school-parking-lots/6929307/.

15. "Mike Pence on Drugs," On the Issues, July 16, 2016, http://www.ontheissues.org/2016/Mike_Pence_Drugs.htm.

16. Megan Twohey, "Mike Pence's Response to H.I.V. Outbreak: Prayer, Then a Change of Heart," *New York Times*, August 7, 2016, https://www.nytimes.com/2016/08/08/us/politics/mike-pence-needle-exchanges-indiana.html.

Chapter 7: Blazing a New Trail

1. Brian Slodysko, "Gov. Mike Pence Facing Tough Re-election After Social Issues Stand," *Indy Star*, May 27, 2016, https://www.indystar.com/story/news/

politics/2016/05/27/gov-mike-pence-facing-tough-re-election-afte-social-issues-stands/85023730/.

2. "Mike Pence Vice President Campaign," Ballotpedia, https://ballotpedia.org/Mike_Pence_vice_presidential_campaign,_2016.

3. Ibid.

4. Jia Tolentino, "Mike Pence's Marriage and the Beliefs That Keep Women from Power," *New Yorker*, March 31, 2017, https://www.newyorker.com/culture/jia-tolentino/mike-pences-marriage-and-the-beliefs-that-keep-women-from-power.

5. Chris Chilliza, "Donald Trump's Interview with '60 Minutes' Was Eye Opening. Also, Mike Pence Was There," *Washington Post*, July 18, 2016, https://www.washingtonpost.com/news/the-fix/wp/2016/07/18/donald-trump-is-way-more-humble-than-you-could-possibly-understand/?utm_term=.c9ade8456d60.

6. Ibid.

7. Roger Stone, *The Making of the President 2016: How Donald Trump Orchestrated a Revolution* (New York: Skyhorse Publishing, 2017), p. 216.

8. Manu Raju, "Tim Kaine: 'I'm a Strong Supporter of Roe v. Wade,'" CNN Politics, July 15, 2016, http://www.cnn.com/2016/07/15/politics/tim-kaine-abortion-roe-v-wade/.

9. "The Vice-Presidential Debate: Tim Kaine and Mike Pence (Full Debate)," NBC News, YouTube video, October 4, 2016, https://www.youtube.com/watch?v=mVXqNcW_-HA.

10. Nicholas Confessore and Matt Flegenheimer, "Vice-Presidential Debate: What You Missed," *New York Times*, October 4, 2016, https://www.nytimes.com/2016/10/04/us/politics/vice-presidential-debate.html.

11. Matthew Tulley, "Tulley: Mike Pence Tries to Clean Up a Messy Weekend," *IndyStar*, October 10, 2016, https://www.indystar.com/story/opinion/columnists/matthew-tully/2016/10/10/tully-mike-pence-tries-clean-messy-weekend/91852634/.

12. April Siese, "Here's the Transcript of Mike Pence's Election Night Speech," *Bustle*, November 9, 2016, https://www.bustle.com/articles/194243-heres-the-transcript-of-mike-pences-election-night-speech.

Chapter 8: White House Bound

1. Roger Stone, *The Making of the President 2016: How Donald Trump Orchestrated a Revolution* (New York: Skyhorse Publishing, New York, 2017), pp. 288, 289.

2. Jason Silverstein, "Here's Who Hillary Clinton Blames for Her Defeat in Campaign Memoir 'What Happened,'" *NY Daily News*, September 12, 2017, http://www.nydailynews.com/news/politics/hillary-clinton-blames-defeat-happened-article-1.3487646.

3. Meghan Keneally and Allie Yang, "Hillary Clinton Opens Up About the Moment She Realized She Lost," ABC News, September 13, 2017, http://abcnews.go.com/US/hillary-clinton-opens-moment-realized-lost/story?id=49817796.

4. Alan Yuhas, "Pence to Head Commission Investigating Baseless Voter Fraud Claim, Trump Says," *Guardian*, February 5, 2017, https://www.theguardian.com/

us-news/2017/feb/05/donald-trump-mike-pence-commission-voter-fraud.

5. Julie Zauzmer and Sarah Pulliam Bailey, "March for Life: Pence Speaks as Thousands Assemble at Washington Monument," *Washington Post*, January 27, 2017, https://www.washingtonpost.com/local/march-for-life-thousands-assemble-at-washington-monument/2017/01/27/7d880d52-e40a-11e6-ba11-63c4b4fb5a63_story.html?utm_term=.ea8bead55879.

6. "John Adams," Whitehouse.gov, https://www.whitehouse.gov/about-the-white-house/presidents/john-adams.

7. "C-32 Air Force Two," Military.com, https://www.military.com/equipment/c-32-air-force-two.

8. Maureen Groppe, "The Perks of Being Vice President," *Indy Star*, January 17, 2017, https://www.indystar.com/story/news/politics/2017/01/17/perks-being-vice-president/96558620/.

9. Theodore Schleifer and Elizabeth Landers, "Pence Visits Jewish Cemetery After Anti-Semitic Attack," CNN Politics, February 22, 2017, https://www.cnn.com/2017/02/22/politics/mike-pence-anti-semitism-cemetery/index.html.

10. Robert Pear and Thomas Kaplan, "House Republicans Unveil Plan to Replace Health Law," *New York Times*, March 6, 2017, https://www.nytimes.com/2017/03/06/us/politics/affordable-care-act-obamacare-health.html.

11. Ryan Struyk, "Mike Pence Is Breaking Ties in the Senate at a Record-Setting Pace," CNN, January 24, 2018, https://www.cnn.com/2017/07/26/politics/

pence-tie-breaking-senate-record-setting-pace/index.
html.

12. Susan Page, "Poll: Most Americans Are Unhappy
with Almost Everyone in Politics—Except
for Mike Pence," *USA Today*, March 7, 2017,
https://www.usatoday.com/story/news/politics/
onpolitics/2017/03/07/suffolk-poll-americans-
unhappy-with-politicians-except-pence/98841138/.

13. "VP Pence to Embark on Asia-Pacific Trip in Mid-
April," VOA News, April 6, 2017, https://www.
voanews.com/a/vp-pence-to-embark-on-asia-pacific-
trip-in-mid-april/3799379.html.

14. Tim Haines, "VP Mike Pence to NASA's 2017
Astronaut Trainees: 'You May Be the First to Travel to
Mars,'" Real Clear Politics, June 7, 2017, https://www.
realclearpolitics.com/video/2017/06/07/vp_mike_
pence_to_nasas_2017_astronaut_trainees_you_may_
be_the_first_to_travel_to_mars.html.

15. Robinson Meyer, "What's Happening with the Relief
Effort in Puerto Rico?" *Atlantic*, October 4, 2017,
https://www.theatlantic.com/science/archive/2017/10/
what-happened-in-puerto-rico-a-timeline-of-
hurricane-maria/541956/.

16. Eric Levenson, "3 Storms, 3 Responses: Comparing
Harvey, Irma, and Maria," CNN, September 27, 2017,
https://www.cnn.com/2017/09/26/us/response-
harvey-irma-maria/index.html.

17. Anita Kumar and Patricia Mazzei, "Pence in Puerto
Rico: We Have a Long Way to Go," Miami Herald,
October 6, 2017, http://www.miamiherald.com/news/
weather/hurricane/article177518681.html.

Chapter 9: No Rest for the Weary

1. Betsy Klein, "Karen Pence Unveils Her Second Lady Platform," CNN Politics, October 18, 2017, https://www.cnn.com/2017/10/18/politics/karen-pence-art-therapy-second-lady/index.html.

2. Mark Landler, "Trump Recognizes Jerusalem as Israel's Capital and Orders U.S. Embassy to Move," *New York Times*, December 6, 2017, https://www.nytimes.com/2017/12/06/world/middleeast/trump-jerusalem-israel-capital.html.

3. Kaitlyn Schallhan, "Why Trump's Promise to Move U.S. Embassy to Jerusalem Is So Controversial," Fox News Politics, February 23, 2018, http://www.foxnews.com/politics/2018/02/23/why-trumps-promise-to-move-us-embassy-to-jerusalem-is-so-controversial.html.

4. Will Gore, "As Donald Trump's Emissary to Israel, Mike Pence Is Looking to a Future in Which He Calls the White House Home," *Independent*, January 22, 2018, http://www.independent.co.uk/voices/mike-pence-donald-trump-jerusalem-israel-embassy-palestinians-middle-east-conflict-presidency-a8172691.html.

5. Katie Leach, "Mike Pence Vows Action on School Safety After Deadly Florida Shooting," *Washington Examiner*, February 17, 2018, http://www.washingtonexaminer.com/mike-pence-vows-action-on-school-safety-after-deadly-florida-shooting/article/2649397.

6. "Vice President Pence and Second Lady Karen Pence Meet North Korean Defectors," Whitehouse.gov, February 9, 2018, https://www.whitehouse.gov/

articles/vice-president-pence-second-lady-karen-pence-meet-north-korean-defectors/.

7. "Pence Slams NK Leader's 'Tyrannical' Sister After Near Meet," MSN.com, February 23, 2017, https://www.msn.com/en-us/news/world/pence-slams-nk-leaders-tyrannical-sister-after-near-meet/ar-BBJsNwt?li=BBnb7Kz.

8. Dwight Adams, "Will Adam Rippon and Mike Pence Ever Talk? Rippon Now Says He's Willing," *Indy Star*, February 24, 2017, https://www.indystar.com/story/news/2018/02/24/mike-pence-and-adam-rippon-ever-talk-rippon-says-hes-willing/370020002/.

9. Ibid.

10. Jonathan Bernstein, "Trump Gets a Piece of Good News," Bloomberg, February 26, 2017, https://www.bloomberg.com/view/articles/2018-02-26/good-news-for-trump-as-approval-rating-rallies.

Glossary

bailout A form of financial aid that is given to a business that is failing.

bicameral A legislative body that is comprised of two parts.

bipartisan When two parties work together toward solutions.

Common Core Clear, developed goals specific to each state and intended to test students and ensure they are on par with those goals.

corporate law Branch of law that deals with corporations and protecting the interests of those corporations.

Federal Election Commission (FEC) Organization in charge of ensuring that federal laws are followed regarding campaign finances.

fraternity Social organization generally formed on college campuses to allow young men to bond through shared interests and experiences.

immigrant A person who has moved from his or her country of birth to a new country with the intention of putting down roots.

impeach To charge a person in public office with improper behavior or misconduct.

infertility The inability to conceive a child.

lobbyist A person who makes it his or her job to try to influence government officials.

think tank A group of people knowledgeable in a specific field who meet to advance ideas regarding that specific area of interest, such as politics or science.

US House of Representatives The lower part of the bicameral Congress whose members create, revise, and repeal legislation that will be in the best interest of their districts.

US Senate The upper part of the bicameral Congress that also attends to lawmaking, but more specifically as it pertains to each senator's state.

Further Reading

Books

Jones, Van. *Beyond the Messy Truth: How We Came Apart, How We Come Together*. New York, NY: Ballantine Books, 2017.

MacLean, Nancy. *Democracy in Chains: The Deep History of the Radical Right's Stealth Plan for America*. New York, NY: Viking, 2017.

Neal, Andrea. *Pence: The Path to Power*. Bloomington, IN: Red Lighting Books, 2018.

Wolff, Michael. *Fire and Fury: Inside the Trump White House*. New York, NY: Henry Holt and Company, 2018.

Websites

Politico
https://www.politico.co
Current trends and breaking reports on all things political.

Factcheck.org
https://www.factcheck.org
Nonpartisan information pertaining to current news.

Index